Sourceness

A Series For Golden Earth Being

Sourceness Mission
www.sourceness.one

Parenting
Book One

Copyright © 2024 Sourceness Mission

The content of this book is the gift of Ascended Masters in service to Source, Earth and humanity through the channels of Sahar Schwaninger and Dr. Lorna Collins. As such it belongs to humanity for their sourceness realisation and we ask that you apply divine discernment and have a conscious intention for the use of any material in this book.

Book cover design and Illustrations are provided to Sourceness Mission by Sylwia Czarneka from WI Design.

Published By: Amazon Publishing Plus.

Acknowledgements

We are grateful to Sahar Schwaninger and Dr. Lorna Collins for their dedication and commitment to providing a pure channelling in service to the Sourceness Mission.

We are thankful to Lanja Fletcher for her generous and detailed proofreading and corrections of the Sourceness manuscripts.

We are thankful to the readers of the Sourceness book series for their curiosity and exploration of the materials gathered in this book.

Telonis, *Master of the Violet Flame of Transmutation on behalf of the Council of Mission Golden Earth.*

Table of Contents

Acknowledgements	4
List of Diagrams	8
List of Tables	9
Introduction	11
PART ONE: FOUNDATIONS: THE HUMAN SYSTEM	20
Chapter 1 The Human Mind & Body System and the Two Levels of Parenting	24
The Simplified Comprehensive View of the Human Body	29
The Detailed Comprehensive View of the Human Body	31
The Human Energy Field or Auric System View	32
The Chakras	36
The Three Minds	38
The Two Levels of Parenting and the Soul-Monadic Structure	39
Your Central Channel: The Antahkarana Bridge	47
Chapter 2 The Parent Light Path and Practice	49
Parenting as a Light Path	49
Navigating in Your Own Rhythm	51
Chapter 3 Universal Consciousness	63
Consciousness and Group Consciousness	63
Chapter 4 Conscious Parenting	72
The Conscious Parent Role	73
Stewardship of the Garden	74
Parenting as an Act of Leadership	74
PART TWO: FOUNDATIONS: GROUNDING & ANCHORING (Anchored-ness)	77
Chapter 1 Grounding and Anchoring for Parents	78
Getting Started	81
Anchoring Your Pillar of Light - Ground and Top	82
Anchoring Your Central Channel	86
Anchoring Your Body System	86
Anchoring Your Earth Star	87

Observing When Your Anchoring/grounding Needs Update	87
Grounding Your Oversoul on Planet Earth	88
Chapter 2 Grounding and Anchoring for Children	89
Patterns of Earth Disconnection with Children	90

PART THREE: THE THREE PILLARS OF PARENTING (Structuredness)   94

Chapter 1 Pillar 1: LOVE / Self Love and Unconditional Love	97
Love at the Personality Level	97
Love at the Soul Level	100
Chapter 2 Pillar 2: WISDOM/Knowledge, Discernment and Divine Wisdom	103
Wisdom at the Personality Level	103
Wisdom at the Soul Level	104
Chapter 3 Pillar 3: POWER / Free Will and Divine Will and Power	106
Power at the Personality Level	107
Power at the Soul Level: Divine Will and Power	109
Conclusion	109

PART FOUR: INTENTIONS OF PARENTING (Intentional-ness)   111

Chapter 1 Constellation	112
What are Divine Light Structures	113
What do we Mean by Constellation	113
Parenting Through Constellations	118
Harmonising Sibling Interactions Through Constellations	120
Conclusion	120
Chapter 2 Cultivating	121
Cultivating Subtle Senses	121
Cultivating Divine Qualities	124
Working with the 12 Planetary Rays	146
How can you Work with Rays as a Parent?	150
Identifying Your Oversoul Ray Type as Parent	150
How Can you Work with the Rays with Your Child?	153

PART FIVE: DELIMITEDNESS   158

Chapter 1 The Language of Parenting	159
Language Delimitation	159
Intentional Sound Vibration	160

Your Language and the Energy of the Rays	160
Calling Forth Your Child's Ideal State	160

Chapter 2 Self-Healing — 162

What is an Ailment?	162
Essential Principles - Guiding Principles	163

Chapter 3 Balancing Polarity — 179

Chapter 4 Parenting your Inner Child and Divine Child — 180

At the Personality Level	180
At the Soul Level	183

Chapter 5 Source and Sourceness — 185

What do we Mean by Source?	185
What do we Mean by Sourceness?	186
Denial of Source	186
Challenges Arise	187
Conclusion	189

List of Diagrams

Diagram 1. Book Structure	16
Diagram 2. Human Energy Bodies	31
Diagram 3. Human Energy Bodies 2	32
Diagram 4. Essential Chakra Connections	35
Diagram 5. Thymus Chamber	36
Diagram 6. Chakras	38
Diagram 7. The Soul - Monadic Structure	43
Diagram 8. The Cosmic Monadic Structure	44
Diagram 9. Integrated Soul Extension into Cosmic Monad	45
Diagram 10. The Antahkarana Bridge 1	48
Diagram 11. The Antahkarana Bridge - Part 2	48
Diagram 12. Auric Levels	67
Diagram 13. Pillar of Light	83
Diagram 14. The Four Bodies	86
Diagram 15. Example of Family Constellation	113
Diagram 16. The Qualities of Parenting	126
Diagram 17. Ray Determination Compass	151
Diagram 18. Oversoul/Monad Ray Determination Compass	152
Diagram 19. Divine Child and Inner Child	180

List of Tables

Table 1 - Chakras - locations and colours	37
Table 2 - Expressions of Consciousness	66
Table 3 - Family Constellations	116
Table 4 - The Rays' Expression Changes	146
Table 5 - The 12 Planetary Rays	146
Table 6 - Main Topics and Learnings on the Path for each Monadic Ray	156

What is Sourceness?

Sourceness is being one within one's Source. It is the experience of Source in this Divine Now Moment. If you try to explain or understand Source, you are in your mind and not experiencing Source. If you are looking for words to speak about Source or describe it, you are restricting Source and not experiencing Source.

Sourceness is being in the now.

Parenting as a Light Path is about embodying your unique expression of Source in this very Divine Now Moment.

At the oversoul level and beyond, you can experience Source, feel Source, be Source and this is the purpose of this book: everyone is able to experience their unique sourceness.

Introduction

Within every adult, there is a child that requires parenting. If you are a parent, then you have not only the child within, but also your children to care for and bring up. In a sense, everyone is a parent: examining, exploring, clarifying and healing limitations of parenting is the topic of this book.

There are currently no comprehensive tools available that enable parenting of self and parenting of one's children in an ideal way for humanity in the context of the great transition we and Earth are experiencing. The foundation of this book is sourceness: this is who we are at the very Source. As we go back to the very core of who we are and re-discover our being, then everything else that is an aspect of who we are - our psyche, our essence, our actions... - can fall into place.

One intention supporting this book is to clarify the path of sourceness - being one within one's Source - and highlight limitations and blockages that we have gathered along the way of our life experiences as individuals and collectives - families, communities, nations...

We provide tools and offer a foundational path towards sourceness, as a new state of being, for all adults of today and tomorrow. While this book has been primarily prepared for parents with children, it will also serve all adults.

Who we are: Sourceness Mission

You will notice that unlike conventional books, there are no named authors in this one. This is to draw attention to the new way of living in Golden Earth where the personality of human beings is no longer central nor even relevant but rather the soul which, coming online, carries its work of service to humanity, planet Earth and Source.

We - soul extensions Sahar Schwaninger and Lorna Collins - have channelled these books through the guidance of our soul and ascended masters who have introduced us to the Sourceness Mission. The work of preparing these books (rather than writing them as is conventionally known) has been one of dedicating ourselves to our personal and spiritual work and continuously refining our channel to receive pure source aligned messages from the various masters who have made themselves available to communicate, supervise, teach and help us progress on our own paths of ascension.

However, nothing about our lives, experiences and learnings is relevant in this book and we have been expressly guided not to put ourselves in here. This was a very clear instruction received which we respected throughout the book preparing project and we continue to do as we continue our work on the following books being prepared in the Sourceness series.

As you will read about personality in this book, you will understand why this is so important: this book is atemporal and universal, it cannot be limited by the finite personalities of Sahar and Lorna or anybody else. It also is not a conversation between you and Lorna/Sahar, but rather between you and Source. So, we put ourselves out of it.

Sahar and Lorna were called by Source (The Source of One's Cosmic Day) to channel and constellate this book. This book is the first of a series of seven books called *Sourceness: A Series for Golden Earth Being.*

As members of the Sourceness Mission, we have been guided to curate this book and the corresponding Sourceness Journal which will assist those who seek a new structure of being in a foundational and practical way. It is our service mission to do so and our intention is to serve the Source of our Cosmic Day, humanity and all of Earth's kingdoms in alignment with divine will.

Our guidance is channelled. Our guide is Source. Numerous other guides (consciousnesses) have come through our channels, and we refer to them throughout this book. We seek to integrate within divine light structures given to us for this book a great deal of information that has been made available to humanity, but not yet structured in a way that allows the integrated experience of sourceness. We have also completed, updated, and amended wherever we have been guided to the previous information shared with humanity. This is not to say that previous information was wrong: it all has to do with the evolution and divine timing of what is made available and serves humanity, Earth and Source.

Likewise, the information in this book will evolve as humanity evolves and new information will be shared. We have realised that as soon as we channel information in the divine present now it becomes 'outdated'. However, we are guided that the energy contained within this book is not constrained in any way. Opening up and accepting to embrace relative truth and live in the divine now moment is part of the way of life in Golden Earth.

We ask you to embrace this book energetically. The energetic encodement within it is in no way personal nor limited. We have made sure, to the best of our ability and with guidance, that it is channelled as purely as possible. This is not a book to read with your analytical mind, but a book to experience.

Dr Lorna Collins and Sahar Schwaninger for Sourceness Mission

Why we Wrote This Book and *Sourceness Journal*

Our guides have made clear to us how important it is now for humanity to begin to accept our divinity, our sourceness: to begin to accept that we are all "divine sparks of Source" having a human experience; to accept and realise that humanity and Earth are one. Those of us on this path will recognize this and this book will serve them.

We wrote this book because we were guided to. We have the possibility today to live our adult lives as spiritually realised humans from a level of integrated consciousness which enables us to experience our sourceness directly.

This is a major shift in consciousness which shatters the old ways through which our societies have been built - fear, hatred, disconnection, segregation, separation, domination...- and invites a total renewal where all can thrive together as one humanity, one Earth. We are collectively paving the road towards the Golden Earth so many of us are yearning for.

The leaders of Golden Earth are the children of today. To prepare for this fundamental shift, there is a need to upgrade our own ways of operating as adults and as parents in the ways we raise our children and parent ourselves. This begins with a fundamental shift in consciousness: we need to examine and reconsider who we are and how we relate to all the various aspects of self.

More than upgrading our understanding, we wrote this book to draw awareness towards a practical new way of being. This book is for today's adults who are parenting the leaders / world servers / citizens of Golden Earth. Today's adults may work with themselves and with their children to grow and integrate higher levels of consciousness needed for the Golden Earth. This book is therefore for all adults as well as parents. It is your choice if it is for you or not.

There is amazing readiness and (spiritual) support available to us at this time to take this next great step in our human journey. This book taps into this support and lays some foundations to align humanity with Golden Earth with practical transition tools that can be used by parents and children.

"When mankind recognizes that they are the Sons of God, that there is divine equality, and that no one is greater than another, then you will have begun your journey in the way that it was intended." [i]

Why you Might Like to Read it

We often think of parenting as adults guiding children into the future. Yet parents are seldom the finished article - meaning that parents are seldom fully god-realised beings. Parents are in the process, on the path, growing towards realising their highest, most complete being.

- What if the children of today had a purpose of guiding the adults into the coming new era, the Golden Earth?
- What if the adults of today could see this as a blessed opportunity to enter on a path of learning, growing and integrating together with their children as they parent?
- What if their children found in their parents open minded adults, willing to put aside what they know from the past?
- What if parents acted like loving companions and guides for their children and supported them to grow up into who they are with the learnings they have brought to teach us?
- What if the answers we need to address our current challenges - ecological, societal, economic, political, spiritual, mental, emotional - were present as seeds of potential within the children of today and came to life in the space of interaction between parent and child?
- What if parents thought of the experience of parenting as a constellation where all are learning and growing together?
- What if adults had within them all the tools, they needed to heal their wounded inner child and become their own ideal parents?

If any of the above is appealing to you or at least stirring your curiosity, then we recommend you read this book. The Golden Earth we envision has nothing to do with the experiences of limitations, lack and fear most humans see as life today. This new way of being is very tangible, awaiting our attention and nourishment to become fully manifested.

We cannot see Golden Earth with the eyes of limitations, fear and separation: we need to go through a process of transformation to see through the eyes of unlimitedness, unconditional love and oneness. This transformation is of a spiritual nature that impacts all the aspects of who you are. If part of you is interested in this transformation, then we recommend you read this book.

What This Book is not

This book does not aim to offer a new paradigm of parenting nor even a new paradigm of being. It is not building upon what already exists with the aim to improve it or criticise it because the foundational consideration we have is that Golden Earth is not built upon wisdom from the past.

This also doesn't mean that wisdom we have learned is not valid. It simply needs to be examined: is this serving Source, humanity, Golden Earth?

The major gap we see today in our societies at large is a profound disconnection from the spiritual aspects of Self and a lack of integration in humanity. Because of these two aspects, this book is profoundly spiritual in nature. When we talk about the domain of soul and Spirit, we are immediately talking about abstract and more or less visible/tangible realms. However, this book is not a new dogma or religion, and it doesn't tap into any religious group consciousness. If anything, we wish the world to be free from any dogmas or precepts. As such, we are not preaching anything, not aiming to make you follow the guidance of this book or change anything in your life. We are simply showing another way of looking at life which is anchored in sourceness. We believe it may serve you, whether you have children or not. We wish to show, describe, and offer experiences of what it means to parent oneself and one's children through the lens of sourceness.

We have no attachment to whether the book serves you or not. We want you to be absolutely free to read this book from your own discernment and adopt what is right for you and leave what is not. All human beings are given free will and this is their divine right, we of course, respect and honour this.

This book is also not claiming that it is the new holy grail to parenting, although we are told by our guidance, that this will radically change the landscape for humanity. Whether this happens through this book, because of this book, in our lifetime or the next, it is not up to us to decide… all is ultimately determined by Source. We have come together with the sole intention to be of service to Source, humanity and Earth, because we are in surrenderedness to Source and in service to humanity and Earth. Humanity can enable a greater vision for Golden Earth or what is called the Golden Age, and our souls are tasked in the mission to enable this.

We are not seeking any personal return, self-aggrandisement, fame, recognition, love, feel good effect or to create a community of belonging - these are all disempowering personality traps which we hold ourselves accountable in our own personal work and throughout the preparing of this book. Our intention is to support humanity, and parents in particular, to become hyper-aware of all the personal and collective disempowering personality traps which are running the show instead of the pure and clear intent of the soul.

This book is also not a list of recipes to apply; instead, it is more of a companion of self-development and parenting. It is like your meditation and self-exploration partner powered by Source. We know that what has brought you to read this book in the first place, will also guide you through using it.

A Word About Updated References

We have mentioned earlier that this book has been channelled through our guides who have tasked us to present information in a specific way which is in divine ideal now for this book. In this process, Lorna was provided with specific instructions to update, clarify or further explain existing information.

We are grateful for the work these dedicated individuals have provided and we are by no means suggesting that the information they have written is not valid. For this book and the intention of providing a path to sourceness as we have been tasked to do, our guides have requested us to acknowledge and update the specific information we have included in this book. We invite you not to read this as a disqualification of previous work or through a dualistic lens that one version is right, and another is not. On the contrary, we are honouring the work we can step on to go further for the purpose of our task. Whenever we have used information in this book which we have updated, precise reference to the author and the initial material is quoted.

Why does this matter? Attention is brought to the human quest and tendency to fix information and see it as "truth" or "untruth". This is a limitation that we are requested to clarify. The moment one fixes something as an absolute truth, one is deviating from the experience of Source.

For example, you may have read about the 7 human chakras, their location and function. Well actually, chakras move as you complete initiations and progress on your spiritual path. When the map of the 7 chakras was shared, the mobility of the chakra system was not relevant, but today, if you believe that your chakras are fixed forever, you will face a limitation on your path. The picture of the seven-chakra system is not wrong, it is however a snapshot which relates to one reality. If you see it as absolute truth, you will limit yourself. As soon as one realises something (the penny drops, we get an A-Ha) one almost immediately needs to let it go. This is a paradox which is at the heart of much spiritual confusion: the moment you hold on to something, you are out of oneness. At the same time, one needs stepping stones to evolve on one's path. The way through this is to apply discernment and this is why we have dedicated a chapter on subtle sensing: one needs a reliable indicator of relative truth which can guide one in each divine now moment.

We highly encourage you to explore for yourself what beliefs you hold about absolute truth, what "truths" you have "written in stone," and envisage that very little is absolute truth and most "absolute truths" become dogma, limiting in nature. The universe(s) is in continuous evolution, Source itself is evolving. We invite you to make peace with being in continuous exploration, evolution, discovery and marvel at the totality of your experience without judging anything and with deep unshakable trust in your soul. For this reason, Sourceness is a series and not one book.

Structure of This Book

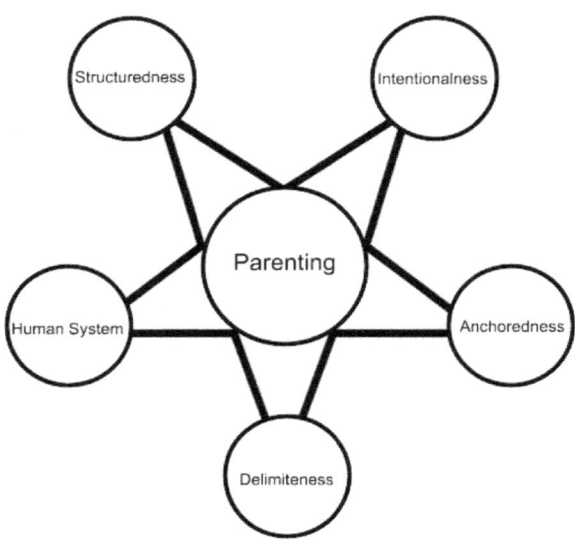

Diagram 1. Book Structure

This book has 5 parts which are based around five themes:
- Human System - the essential understanding of what the human system comprises.
- Structuredness - everything in the infinite universe is structured.
- Intentionalness - intention achieves and does everything in our world.
- Anchoredness - connecting our multi-dimensional being to relevant reality.
- Delimitedness - the theme until 2035 is Era of Unlimitedness so collectively our soul work is to delimit our being.

The *Sourceness Journal*

In some cultures, it is popular to diarize or journal the journey of the newborn baby through childhood. Baby albums are sold for this purpose. They offer the opportunity to record information, pictures, images, and important mementos of the baby's early life. We continue to save mementos, record experiences as they grow.

The *Sourceness Journal* that accompanies this book comes from these traditions. In it we invite you to record your journey as a parent guide along with your child's journey as together you develop and grow together as a family.

The *Sourceness Journal* is for both parent and child. It includes multiple and diverse exercises, reflections, practices... for you to find a variety of ways to converse with yourself, your soul and enter a soul-to-soul parenting relationship with your child. It also contains exercises and practices to explore with your child, and the exercises and practices just for your child. So, it is equally relevant for both parent and child as you evolve together. For every chapter you read in the book, there is a dedicated section in the *Sourceness Journal*.

The Golden Earth and the Golden Age

We have mentioned this notion of the Golden Earth a few times already. Let us explain what we mean by this and what it is not.

A few years ago, Earth underwent a spiritual upgrade which has fundamentally shifted the way it operates. Earth, just like us, is a living being on a spiritual journey. Earth is our (humanity) planetary body. So, we are inherently intertwined, interwoven.

As a result of this upgrade which you can see as Earth's awakening, some of the ways of humanity are no longer supported and need adjustment. These are some aspects which currently need upgrading:
- The sense of separation between beings,
- The greed, abuse, violation and domination of human beings over themselves and other beings on Earth,
- The hoarding and frenetic materialism of the current human civilisation,
- The egoistic focus of human civilisation and identification with lower mind, body and emotions,
- The disempowering myths humans live by and promote,
- The attachment to material belongings and identification to matter,
- The negation and denial of the divine in humanity,
- The cause and effect thinking characteristic of the lower mind,
- The human basis of operation from 3D to 5D,
- The limitations of mass/collective consciousness.

The upgrading processes are already underway in the Golden Earth. We will experience a new Golden Age for humanity where the embodiment of greater light into humanity's physical body systems and the integration of the spiritual bodies will literally make human bodies radiate a halo of golden light - this is partially where the name comes from. This is a process of spiritualising matter and shifting from the density of lower vibrations to higher ones: the Golden Age is about radiating golden light consciously and this implies the recognition that one is golden light. This book provides frameworks and tools to align with the Golden Earth.

It is useful to also mention what Golden Earth is not: so many well-intended human beings on a spiritual path or a path of service to others are longing for a future where there is no suffering, where they can be at peace, where they experience harmony and unconditional love. How could we not yearn for this? We inherently know how love, light, equity, justice... feel like. The challenge and limitation of this is that the yearning is rooted in fear, stemming from the current experience of pain, hurt, darkness, inequity, injustice... Golden Earth is not a future we imagine to 'run away' from the limiting state we experience today. It comes about through the transformation of our limitations.

This does not mean that you cannot envision, imagine, align yourself with Golden Earth, on the contrary, the power of imagination is an engine for manifestation. However, it is essential that all envisioning of Golden Earth is rooted in Golden Earth, in unlimitedness and not in limitations. This is also why this era is called the Era of Unlimitedness.

A Word on Universal Laws and Basic Laws of Life

As above, So Below; As Within, So Without
This law states that patterns of vibration / light / energy repeat throughout the quantum universe, and on a personality level, our reality is a mirror of what's happening within and without us in every divine now moment. When we feel ready to receive from the Universe, we ask calmly and sincerely, e.g., 'Please may I have all the help I need to be an ideal parent.' The Universe is here to help us: it will be delighted that we have asked and will help us. The help may not always arrive in the way we 'think' it should. However, if we value help in whatever form it takes, we may be pleasantly surprised at how often it arrives. The Universe rearranges itself to reflect our (personality level) reality. Literally what we believe is real within us, will be our experience/reality without.

The Law of Request
If we wish help from the Universe, Source, angelic realm, from Spirit in all its forms, we must ask for it. Help cannot be provided by the Universe unless we request it. It is also the case that helping others needs to be in response to their request for help. If we see / sense / feel / know that someone needs help, remind them that help is infinitely available if they ask. If they or you do not know what to ask for... 'please help me' is sufficient. Sometimes we can become too specific in our request for help and that can limit the help available. We don't always have

to know exactly what help we need. We all have free will at the personality level. To take that away from another is to violate universal law, so help others if they ask, do not assume they wish/seek help. Of course, if one is in distress or is unable to ask for help, love prevails. That is, do what is unconditionally loving, do what love (God-self) would do.

Law of Attraction
The Law of Attraction states that like attracts like, and that we get/become what we focus on, what we transmit. Not only that, but we must believe / accept / allow that what we wish to attract is possible in the first instance. We become what we focus on. All the vibrations that we radiate, our light radiance, is made up of conscious and unconscious energy. All electrons within our energy systems are charged. Some of the charges are attractors (to some), some repel (to some), some are neutral, and everything in between.
The universe provides a mirror - the universe is holographic.

Law of Resistance
We become what we resist. Whatever we resist persists in our life and uses our energy in struggle until we release it, let it go. Resist nothing, welcome everything.

Law of Reflection
Everything in the universe(s) – and yes there is more than one universe – is a reflection. Whatever comes into, or is in, your life, look into the mirror and see what it reflects to you. Source is always helping us. Look within.

Law of Projection
We often project our stuff onto other people and assume it is within them, often denying it is with us. We do not, necessarily, know how anyone feels or is. Of course, if you are clairvoyant or claircognizant you may well 'know' or 'sense'. Everything we see in another is a projection of an aspect of oneself. Until it isn't. The focus on the personality level is a foundational requirement for us all. Begin here. Our life is what we experience. It is not necessary or helpful to judge others. Other people probably experience a similar life very differently. Taking responsibility for our own emotions is important. Going within to process them is essential and offers enormous opportunities for spiritual growth.

Law of Attachment
You may have anything you wish in life, but if your sense of self-worth or happiness depends on having it, then we are attached to it. Whatever or whomever we are attached to has the ability to manipulate us – so we lose our freedom – and we become controllable by that which we are attached to. Detachment from attachment is a precursor to freedom to be all that we already are.

Law of Divine Oneness or the Law of One

This law highlights the interconnectedness of all things. Beyond our conscious sensing, every thought, energy, action and experience is connected to everything in the Universe. To embody this, we are guided to embrace our connection to our soul/oversoul, be compassionate with all, and recognize that we are all One.

Law of Vibration

This law is that at the quantum level everything is in constant motion, vibrating at specific frequencies. This applies to all Spirit and all matter in the universe. As each of us is composed o electrons and particles we are a collection of vibrating electrons. Our vibrational frequency informs our lived experience.

PART ONE: FOUNDATIONS - THE HUMAN SYSTEM

Becoming a parent is seen by many as a natural step in human life and yet, the arrival of a child in an adult household is so often described as revolutionary. From *"I didn't know what love is before I held this little being in my hands"* to *"if I had been warned of what it means to be a parent, I am not sure I would have signed up for it!"* and everything in between, the experience of parenting can be profound and significant. On the practical level, it touches upon everything, from your schedule and life organisation to your activities, lifestyle, eating and sleep patterns, available time for self / couple/ family / friends, work time… All of these bring about questions to reflect upon with yourself and your partner.

On a deeper personal level, becoming a parent also brings about questions you may not have examined or only partially examined and may not have clear or full answers to: what is your calling? What values do you want to transmit? What type of home are you creating? What type of parent will you be? Are you aligned with your parent partner? What personal limitations do you have that you want to transform?

As you start opening to such questions, the soul level kicks-in and offers new questions: What is a fulfilling life to you? Why are you here on Earth? Who are you? What is your mission? Why are you called to be a parent? What is parenting? Who is the child you will parent? Why is that child coming into your life? What are the learnings your soul is pursuing? What is serving this child? Etc… Etc…

In the face of the breadth and depth of questions parents are faced with, a solid foundation in spirituality is essential so that one has the structure and tools to access within the answers one seeks. The aim of this part is to share a comprehensive yet simple summary of the spiritual aspects of Self and clarify what we mean by parenting through the lens of sourceness.

We wish that parenting is not a bittersweet "something" that happens to you or that you figure out *"à tâtons"* through your blood and sweat as you walk through it, but rather a joyful experience of growth and integration into greater love, light and wisdom. In this sense, parenting becomes a conscious part of both parent and child soul journeys.

> *"You went out in search of gold, far and wide.
> But all along, You were gold In the inside."* Rûmi

The Metaphor and Image of the Garden

One of our primary intentions in this book is to support parents in creating a healthy, fertile and joyful home for themselves and their children, and by home we mean both the literal home in which you live as a family, but also the metaphoric one within yourself.

We see parenting like gardening: consciously caring, mending, nurturing and enjoying a garden where you plant seeds you want to see grow. A garden is alive, it is a piece of Earth with the essence of the beings living in it under the stewardship of the gardener. A gardener listens to the needs of the beings living in the garden, is moved by love, and follows the guidance season after season. This is what we mean by gardener.

We invite you, parent, to see yourself as this gardener, moved by unconditional love, listening day after day to what is ideal for your child's soul, for their radiance to emerge and shine forth, for their integration in their physical incarnation, for the learning they wish to make and the evolutionary path they wish to experience.

There are many ways to garden. The conventional way is to follow the experience of others before you, reading books, listening to expert advice, collecting recipes and trying out...

There is another way which we are offering in this book: it is not feeding the present moment or NOW with learnings from the past. On the contrary, it is anchored in this present now and taps into what we call the Divine. In the following chapters, you will read about what this means in more detail.

When we meet the NOW with preconceived ideas and automatic thinking/behaving, we cannot access its full potential, we cannot experience our full potential or that of our child, or that of the situation. It is not to say that there is a parenting style that is better than another, but rather our intention is to open and include a wider lens to parenting.

A garden is a living organism and in every Divine NOW Moment, there is potential for unlimitedness within the divine structures at play. Have you ever considered yourself as a divine structure? Your family as a divine constellation?

Everything about your growth comes from within you as you evolve through life and make your human experiences. Just like the perfection of the tree is already in the seed.

So instead of gardening the conventional way, we are offering another way of looking at your garden and nourishing it which is anchored in sourceness.

Who are you?

We invite you to read this excerpt with your complete attention and focus - receive it as an energetic message rather than intellectual.

"Thoughts and feelings are living vibrating realities. When you understand this, you can use the higher mind to control yourself and our reality accordingly. When you decide to manifest and experience through consciously directed visualisation, you become the law of the One, God, to whom there is no opposite.

You are a being with free will. You must make your own decision and then stand behind your own decree with all your power - making an unshakable, determined stand. Know that through you, it is God desiring, God feeling, God knowing, God manifesting and God controlling everything. This is the law of the One — Source and Source only.

When this is fully understood, the individual can succeed in manifestation. The moment a human element enters the scenario, it is taken out of the I Am Presence, Source, neutralized by the human qualities of time, space and many other illusory conditions that God does not recognize - conditions that are created by man and man alone.

If one considers that any force other than God exists, then one can never know God; for whenever one acknowledges that two forces can act, you experience the result of neutralizing activity. When you have neutralization, you have no definitive quality either way; you merely have nothing in your manifestation.

When you acknowledge your Source as self — the One, the I Am Presence — you have only perfection manifesting instantly, in a state where there is nothing to oppose or neutralise it, and no element of time.

When you express yourself as God, there is nothing to oppose you and your desire. Only when you truly desire the ideal and cease to acknowledge any power outside of God do you immeasurably improve your condition." [ii]   What if the central intention of your life were to experience fully, completely, unshakably, in every divine now moment your I am presence? To know, feel, sense, see irrefutably, that you are Oneness?

You Are

We invite you to read the following message channelled through Mahatma, from Undifferentiated Source / the One. Allow for the pure Source energetic encoding in it to work with you, move through you and align you with Oneness. You may consciously call on Mahatma, the avatar of synthesis, to be with you as you read this message.

Message from THE ONE through Mahatma: The Law of One

You are one (human god-self), and one is God.
God is ONE (Undifferentiated Source - US).
One alone chooses which qualities and forms one wishes to place in one's world.
One is the only energizer of one's life.
Whenever one thinks or feels, part of one's life force - one's radiance - goes out to sustain one's creation. Goes out to sustain ONE's experience.
One is the Creator (ONE) represented on the universal level.
If one desires to express its perfection and dominion one must know and acknowledge the Law of the ONE. The ONE exists and expresses everywhere, in the universal and monadic levels.
One is part of the ONE supreme presence, the great flame of love and light that is the self- consciousness of life.
Fully acknowledge one's God-self. One's world is the expression of the ONE. Hold this focus in one's daily life.
one and ONE - there is no distinction between them.
Be in Now.
When you are doing visualisation, always remember that one is God doing the picturing, one is God intelligence directing, one is God power propelling, and it is one's substance — God substance — being activated.
Have no set time in your mind, except to know that there is only now.

Free Will

Human beings have free will by design: this is a universal law which states that all human beings have the right to choose their own actions and decisions. You make a decision and learn from its consequences. It is entirely up to you what you think, what you feel, what you believe in, and what conclusions you make of an experience, what experiences you choose to have... Source will not intervene and will not judge your choices.

There is a chapter dedicated to will and power. For now, we would like to stress that this book and all the recommendations and tools we are offering are anchored in specific use of free will, which we believe is the ideal use of free will: the use of free will in alignment with divine will for one's highest well-being and the benefit of all. Let us unpick this and explain why we recommend this:

- When you align your free will to divine will, you are tuned to your divine wisdom and power. To be in your sourceness, this is needed. Source/God is not a high-power outside of you, it is who you are in your pure core.
- When your intention is focused towards your highest well-being in alignment with divine will, you are activating your highest potential of health, love, wisdom and power.

- What is aligned with divine will for your highest well-being is in the benefit of all because all is Source.

We could shorten this statement to "in alignment with divine will" because divine will includes your highest well-being in the benefit of all. However, we are guided that at this stage, it is beneficial to use the full statement. Everything in this book is prepared in alignment with divine will, for your highest well-being and the benefit of all.

The Gift and Commitment of Parenting

That you have agreed to parent a child into this world is a magnificent decision you took. It is indeed a truly noble act of collaboration in service to the collective. By becoming a parent, you have confirmed your commitment to serve: the child who comes under your adult responsibility, planet Earth who is calling these children to life, and to Source. This is a much wider sense of Service than the conventional view on parenting which stems from the psychological lens.

Parenting through the eyes of Source is a spiritual endeavour and we invite you in this book to step up to that spiritual window over your life. Your parenting engagement is primarily from your soul to the soul of your child. The consequences of such a realisation and commitment are manifold, and they fundamentally impact the way you prioritise your and your child's life; how you make sense of what you experience in your life and within you; how you interact with yourself, each other and others; how you live at large.

As your child grows up, by holding your commitment to parent from "soul to soul", you have the choice to put emphasis on the spiritual realisation of your child and not only his/her psychological realisation. This is of great service: your child is already connected to his/her soul at birth and when it undergoes the conditioning of school and society, your help can ensure that the soul connection remains. Your own interactions with him/her will also determine the focus that your child will put on soul versus mass consciousness / consensus reality. As a parent and while the child is under your guidance, you can also play a fundamental role in clearing the confusions and limitations your child carries from other lifetimes.

Through the "soul to soul" parenting principle, you are also committing to supporting your child to expand his/her awareness of him/herself as a soul and make his/her life decisions and
experiences based upon it. This involves a continuous observation of who your child is and the clearing of your projections, conceptions, expectations and limitations on them to approach them in a detached way. For example, what is beneficial to your child may have nothing to do with what is beneficial to you, and the experiences that your child is meant to have may not be yours at all.

Parenting through the lens of Source is a magnificent gift to yourself, your child and humanity. But also, as we mentioned earlier, it is also a great service to our planet and Source.

Channelled Message from the Mahatma Energy
- Avatar of Synthesis

Dear parents, thank you for bringing the children to life. Your role as parents is essential in the empowerment of these children who are meant to bring about the new world.

Dear children, thank you for coming to life. Your energy, vibration and freedom to operate are much needed in this time of extraordinary shift for the Earth which is profoundly impacting humanity.

The changes that you are experiencing on Earth are unique. They hold the possibility for unprecedented growth and integration in consciousness in ways that can liberate you in a lifetime. These changes will radically impact how you live on this planet, how you lead your lives, how you interact with one another, what your priorities are and every aspect of being human.

Channelled Message from the Mahatma Energy
- Avatar of Synthesis

Dear parents, at this moment in your human evolution, changes are taking place so rapidly that a whole new way of upbringing/nurturing is needed. For the old ways cannot exist in the Golden Earth and these old ways are already rooted in the way you bring your children up, from the very moment of conception to the various stages of childhood.

The old ways are imprinted in you as parents, and they determine how you conceive the roles of parents and child and how you operate. All the limitations of your subconscious mind need to be released for you to parent the children of Golden Earth. Your soul has already agreed to it and this book is here to help you consciously act upon your commitment.

The old ways are also imprinted in the children from their own karma, other life experiences and the limitation programming that they have carried into this incarnation. Also, the children face the challenge of operating at much higher/finer vibration than the world is currently operating at - especially the social structures and habits are not adapted to their needs, creating much discomfort in their nervous system and in their ability to integrate the daily exposure to stressors. These children also operate on a much more elaborate template than previous generations and much of the wisdom we need to access and develop is already fact for them. However, they need our support to integrate their spiritual growth into their bodies, to bring what they already know in their conscious awareness.

Before we can present some of the tools we wish to share with you, we need to have a common understanding of the grounds we are operating on. This requires a revisit of who you think you are as a human being, as a parent and as a child. It also requires that we can use a common language, including when referring to concepts that are not easily put into words.

February 28th, 2023

The Templates and the Challenge of Generations

Every human being is operating on the divine human template - monadic blueprint - maya-varupa body which is true for all human beings: we are all one humanity. For example, we all have a physical heart that pumps blood for the system, we have lymph that nourishes the blood; we all have emotions and thoughts; we all aspire to grow… It is a bit like the software on your mobile phone which rules the entire operating system.

However, everyone one of us is running on our own unique version of a blueprint at the oversoul level. Groups of individuals, usually of a given timeframe, share the same template set-up. To use the analogy of the mobile phone, some groups are running on IOS version 1.1 and others on IOS version 2.1… (numbers are irrelevant). This is important for you to consider because of the gap in generational set-up.

There are many energetic templates and what follows is an oversimplification, but for the purpose of this book, we would like to stress three groups:

The group of **currently mature adults (currently above 35)** are, operating on a range of templates which makes them more identified with their earthly existence than their spiritual nature. They see themselves and the world through the lens of limitations and constraints of physicality with their souls' intention to predominantly experience challenges and learnings related to lack, separation, power loss, denials, disconnection from love and loneliness through the experience of earthly challenges. For example, "there is not enough / I am not enough" or "life is a struggle for survival". That soul journey is about returning to Source by awakening to the spiritual aspects of Self. This group is, generally speaking, over-identified with the material.

The group of **younger generations of adults (currently between 21 and 30)** are on a set of different templates, which are close to the one of the older groups with the difference that their soul journey is more about anchoring on Earth and remembering their Earthly nature rather than escaping in the spiritual realms and avoiding the challenges of material life. In comparison, they are over-identified with the spiritual and find earthly living difficult because it is too limiting to their infinite dreams. Their souls' intention is to predominantly experience the challenges and learnings related to accepting matter, grounding and anchoring on Earth, and learning to balance the material and the spiritual in their lives.

The group of Children (currently below 14) are, in general, on yet another set of templates: while their parents must work to open up to their spiritual nature and remember that they are divine in essence, these children are already massively open to their spiritual aspects. Consequently, they are exposed to numerous experiences which generate imbalances and even put them sometimes at risk, impeding their ideal functioning in daily life. Some aspects of the so-called 'new' "learning disabilities", such as dyslexia, dysgraphia, dyscalculia… and "mental health disorders" such as ADHD or ADD are related to the set-up of the child's template and can be heavily improved through dedicated work on the template.

Some aspects of these currently called "disabilities" or "disorders" are the new norm on which these children are meant to thrive for the upcoming era. This topic requires particular attention from parents as we suspect (and are told) that many of the readers of this book have such children. We encourage you to read and practise the exercises related to the template set-up in the *Sourceness Journal,* as well other practices which are particularly effective for highly sensitive children.

What is the difference between this template and the previous one? Unlike the young adult's template described above, this template is at ease with both the spiritual and the material: the challenge is in the adjustment. The grounding challenges these children experience are not due to an overidentification with the spiritual, but rather the lack of tools to help them anchor a much greater spiritual energy into Earth than is currently known. These children are called by Earth to help complete its spiritualisation process. Much of their soul mission is linked to helping Earth.

Chapter 1
The Human Mind & Body System and the Two Levels of Parenting

Throughout time, we have come to understand that parenting is not only physical, but also emotional, psychological, social/relational, energetic, spiritual… We have also experienced how none of these aspects are isolated but seem to interact with each other. However, we are missing a structure to navigate these aspects in a clear way. As an increasing number of people are evolving their consciousness, it becomes more relevant to include the spiritual bodies into the understanding of "body." Also, many terms are being currently used in different ways, creating confusion. So, we would like to map the terminology we will use in this book and use one common language. We are not saying that this language is better, especially because the view of the human energetic system evolves as one evolves on their human journey. There is not a fixed "anatomy of spirit". However, for the purpose of navigation, clarity and simplicity, we choose to fix a view in this book that corresponds to the evolutionary stage of soul extensions working towards the integration of their oversoul (you will read in greater details about these terms and what they mean). In the coming chapters, we will investigate the various views of the human body system, the three minds, and the two levels of parenting which we will refer to and work within this book.

The Simplified Comprehensive View of the Human Body

This view sees the human system in four bodies:

1) **The physical body:** The physical vehicle of incarnation of the human being on planet Earth. It is manifested matter such as cells, organs, blood. The physical body is the one we most commonly identify with because we can see / sense / feel / hear it.

    Our physical body is composed of cells, and it may be helpful to think of the physical body as a universe unto itself, each of us is God of our own universe. There are two parts to the physical body - the dense physical and the etheric which is a layer around our physical shell.

2) **The emotional (astral) body:** This body extends beyond the physical body. The emotional body contains emotions, the feelings one has about oneself. One's feelings and emotions about oneself (person level) flow through this body. The emotional body enables us to feel our thoughts in a tangible manner. The emotional body requires clearing, as do all bodies, if one is to achieve integration leading to spiritual development and higher consciousness. The ideal for this body is 100% unconditional self-love.

    From the emotional body we give and express love and caring, thus fulfilling needs to be in relationships. We feel anger and frustration in this body when our needs are not met. Our emotional body is demanding, seeking fulfilment through experience.

Emotions and feelings are energy vibrating - when we change vibration, we change our emotions and feelings.

3) **The mental body:** The mental body extends beyond the emotional body, is composed of fine light substance/energy, all of which is associated with thoughts and mental processes, and comprehension of conceptual forms and structures. As one clears this body of limiting thoughts and concepts, this body expands in constant motion and movement.

Through our mental body we expose ourselves to knowledge: through reason and logic we apply that knowledge. It is also this body that holds rigid attitudes and structures. The more fluid our mental body, the easier it is to flow with life, the easier it is to change 'our ways of living' and accept new ideas.

4) **The spiritual body:** This body extends beyond the mental body and contains the energetic substance of relationship - the I-Thou connection. It has been described that the spiritual body contains all the love and joy, as well as all the struggle and pain, of relationship. The reason for this is because we lodge pain and struggle within this body... in its pure state the spiritual body is pure love and pure joy. The spiritual body extends well beyond the physical body, and as one clears it of limitations and density, it expands.

Each energetic body interpenetrates the bodies around it. So even though the diagram below shows the bodies as distinct layers from each other, they are not in reality like this. The bodies are also not equal in size - the bodies move constantly in the divine present now moment, so they expand and contract constantly for most people. When the bodies have achieved a level of integration and coherence they fluctuate in size less.

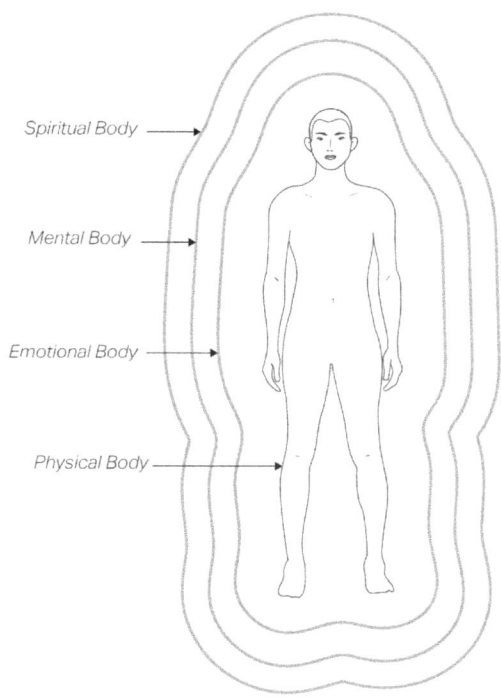

Diagram 2. Human Energy Bodies

The Detailed Comprehensive View of the Human Body

This view is a zoom from the above structure into the next granularity level which enables us to access the etheric aspect of Self:

1) **The physical body:** as above.
2) **The etheric body:** This body is closely linked to the physical; it is an etheric web surrounding the physical body, enabling through energetic centres known as chakras, the energetic transmissions, adjustments and upgrades from the spiritual bodies, into the physical body, but also from the physical body towards the spiritual bodies. It is an interface which also connects one to the astral plane.
3) **The emotional body:** as above.
4) **The mental body:** as above.
5) **The lower mind:** is also called the subconscious mind. It is sometimes referred to as the "Thinker."
6) **The higher spiritual bodies:** There are numerous bodies beyond which nest the oversoul and monadic bodies in their physical, emotional and mental aspects.

Sourceness: A Series for Golden Earth Being

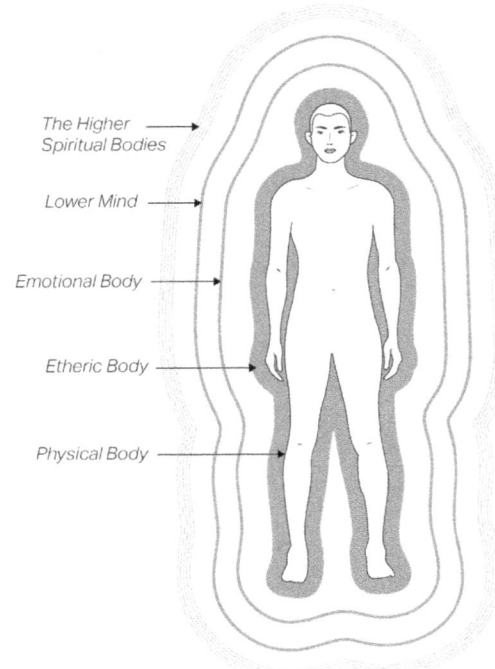

Diagram 3 – Human Energy Bodies 2

The Human Energy Field or Auric System View

This view sees the human body system through the lens of the aura which is, for example, used by healers to identify imbalances and disease in the person or in their relationships.

The auric field is conventionally described as an energy field surrounding the physical body comprised of seven layers:

The first layer: within this layer, you feel all physical sensations.
The second layer: is associated with feelings and emotions about yourself.
The third layer: is associated with our mental or rational world.
The fourth layer: carries our whole world of relationships. From this layer, we interact with other people, animals, plants, inanimate objects, the earth, the sun, the stars and the universe. It is the level of the "I-Thou" connection.
The fifth layer: this is the layer of divine will. Divine will exists within you and all around you and you can access it in this layer. You have free will to either align yourself with this will or not. Divine will is a template or pattern for the great evolutionary plan of humanity and the universe.
The sixth layer: is the layer of feelings within our divine love and spiritual ecstasy.

The seventh layer: is the layer of the divine mind. It serves to hold the entire field together. When we bring our conscious awareness to this layer, we experience divine mind within us and enter the world of the universal divine mind field. If the seventh layer is strong, charged and healthy, your two major abilities will be to have creative ideas and to clearly understand broad overall concepts about existence, the world and its nature.

These views may seem different, but they complement each other. It is a matter of perspective. We will refer to these views in the various tools we will use in this book.

The Human Energy System - Is connected to and interacts with divine light structures

What is the Thymus?

The thymus gland is in the chest, between the lungs and behind the breastbone or sternum. It is just in front of and above the heart.

The thymus gland grows to its largest size during childhood and makes all the T cells we need before we become teenagers. After this, it gradually gets smaller, becomes less active and is replaced by fatty tissue. T cells are a type of white blood cell and are part of the immune system and develop from stem cells in the bone marrow. T cells help protect the body from infection.

Why is the Thymus Important?

"The soul, when it anchors into the physical, anchors as far into the physical as possible, which is right into the physical body. Since chakras are in the etheric body, where in the physical body does the soul go?

"It touches into that organ most closely associated with the heart chakra. We do not mean the physical heart, the heart pump; we mean the thymus gland. The thymus is that gland, a part of the endocrine system which works with energy by transmuting it from an electrical impulse into a more chemical substance within the body. The function of the endocrine system is to transmute the energy from the higher levels, stepping it down into a more basic, concrete, physical level."

"The thymus gland is a key element in that it acts as the seat of the soul in the physical body. Also, within the etheric body at Soul Merge is that eighth chakra, the Soul Star. So, the soul has a two-pronged connection."

"The Thymus Chakra / gland / thymus chamber is also known as the Higher Heart. The Higher Heart and the Soul Star and the Throat Chakra work together in a constellation." [iii]

The Higher Heart

The Higher Heart serves the following purposes:

Connects to Divine Truth: It helps you define your truth born from the desires of your soul found in your heart, and this helps you define your intention and express this in your Throat chakra. It opens your awareness to your truth and inner soul wisdom.

Forms Intent: This energy centre is the connection between the reason for language and the expression of emotions of the heart. It is what makes you take a deep breath before you speak consciously, and form the intent behind your words before you speak them. It is the gateway to higher consciousness, which is based on love, and therefore, a life of abundance, prosperity, joy and satisfaction.

Enhances Immunity: When energised, this centre aids your thyroid gland, throat health, and immune system, bringing protection to the emotional, mental, and spiritual layers of your aura by dispelling unbalanced energy.

Connects Divine Love and Divine Power: The Higher Heart centre connects you to the higher frequency emotions of Divine Love, Joy, Bliss, Gratitude, Compassion, Peace, Acceptance, personal truth from your heart and soul, Forgiveness, and release of fear. It allows you to speak your truth from your spiritual/cosmic heart with compassion, and to understand and manifest your oversoul and monadic blueprint. It also connects you to the divine within you – the divine spark in your first/lower heart, which also empowers your truth and your compassion to your oversoul.

Connects to Healing Power of Divine Love: Connects you to divine love – ultimate Source in the universe. When you are fully connected to all that you are, you can radiate through your being / four bodies all that one is – the Mighty I am Presence.

Connects to Ascension Energies: The heart, like all chakras, is an etheric multi-dimensional space. Consider there is an elevator, you can ride up and ascend to higher levels of one's heart. The Higher Heart is an access point - the reception room to one's vast inner universe. When you move up into the higher frequencies of your heart, you expand your awareness of All That Is, and have greater awareness of your soul blueprint and mission and much more.

What is the Thymus Chamber

The thymus chamber is the welcome centre for the Higher Heart / Thymus Chakra, but it isn't quite the same as other chakras. It is a gateway, a portal into the inner world, the inner god-self. It looks like a large chamber - or it will do when activated - or reception area - welcome space. The inner world space of the god-self, for most, looks like a vast palace with suites of rooms in various decor and configurations.

Why this is so is to make it easier for us to navigate when we are just beginning to master our subtle sensing abilities. The absolute truth is everything is patterns of light, colour, vibration and sound. Somewhat psychedelic so difficult for the lower mind to comprehend.

We are guided to work with the Higher Heart from the thymus chamber because to soul merge (you will read later about this), one needs to get the Higher Heart and Soul Star chakras activated and online. We encourage you to visualise your thymus chamber as a beautiful golden room, lit with liquid golden light, and containing your throne of divinity and sovereignty in its centre on a dais. Your throne is substantial, golden, light, solid, calm. You enter the thymus chamber through the Higher Heart, by bringing your attention there and setting your intention. We encourage you to enter this chamber and sit there, on your throne of divinity and sovereignty, breathing pure light and with your intention, filling the chamber with pure light.

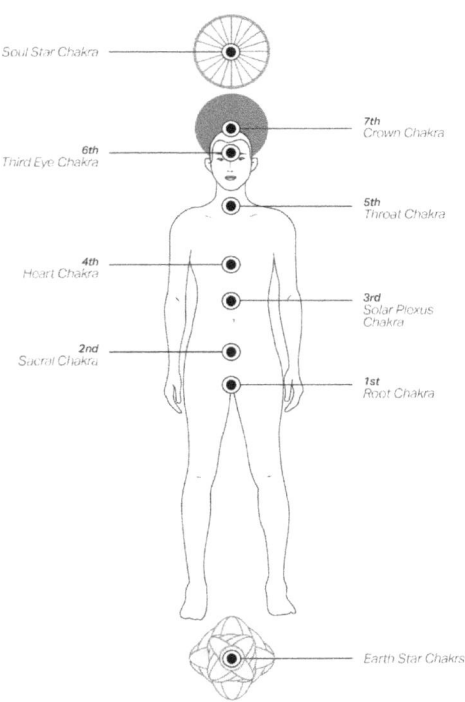

Diagram 4. Essential Chakra Connections

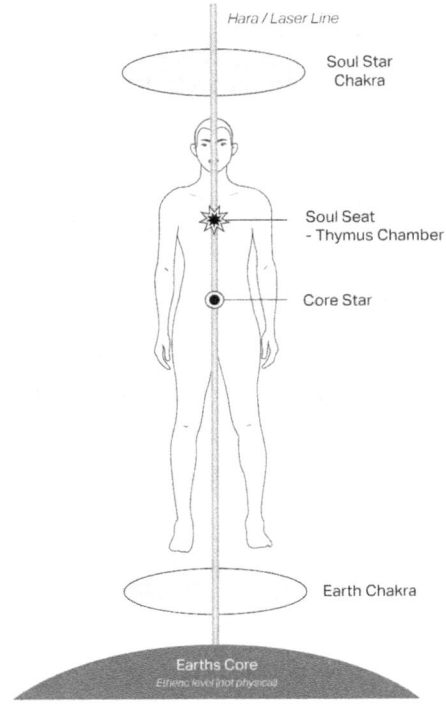

Diagram 5. Thymus Chamber

The Chakras

For completeness we include a short introduction to chakras. Much has been written and there are many resources to read and watch about chakras and we encourage you to become familiar with them in your own etheric body - the chakras are in the etheric body not the physical. This is foundational knowledge. Some people use numbers to name chakras, others use Western traditional names and some Sanskrit names. In this book we use western traditional names.

Chakras are energy centres, and vortices, channels through which energy flows in and out of the physical body. Most literature discusses the seven main chakras but we each have hundreds located all over the body. The energy which flows through the chakras comes from inside and outside the chakras. The chakras radiate energy. The chakras receive energy.

Remember we exist in an ocean of energy. Electrons and infinitely small particles as yet unknown to scientists surround us, are us. Electrons have a core of PURE SOURCE surrounded with an aura of charged energy - just like us. The aura of electrons is charged with energy, everything from unconditional love, compassion, care to hatred, anger, distrust, etc. We exist in this ocean of electrons all with auras charged with energy.

Until one is aware of this, one may choose to 'protect' one's being from energies that do not serve one. One focuses in the beginning on what serves one or what does not serve one. This beginning stage is where protection from non-serving energies is helpful to employ.

Why is it helpful? It is helpful because the awareness of the 'chargedness' of energy serves us in developing our ability to discern our own energy and the energy of others. It is helpful so we begin to see / sense / feel / know / hear what is serving us and what is not. Again, in the beginning this is helpful until we can manage our energy, release it in a way that is ideal and radiate what is ideal.

Realise that all energy serves and all is created by THE ONE (God - Source). All energy serves in some way. Even if we are not conscious of how or why it serves, it is not accidental - it is as the divine wills. There is no negative energy - there is energy which does not serve one, or energy which is not aligned with divine ideal. There is no positive energy - there is energy that serves one, or energy which is aligned to divine ideal.

Let go of judgement. We direct you to the resources section and the Sourceness Journal for further information to study about one's chakras.

Table 1 - Chakras - locations and colours

Number	Western Tradition Name	Sanskrit Name	Location	Colours
1	Root/base	Mudlahara	Coccyx - base of spine	red
2	Sacral/Polarity	Svadhighthana	Mid-point below navel	orange
3	Solar Plexus		Solar plexus	yellow
	Navel/Manipu-	Manipura	Navel	orange
4	Heart	Anahata	Centre of chest	green
5	Throat	Visudha	Centre of throat	blue
6	Brow/3rd Eye	Ajna	Between eyebrows	indigo
	5th Eye		Centre of Forehead	rainbow
7	Crown	Sahasrara	Top of head	violet/purple

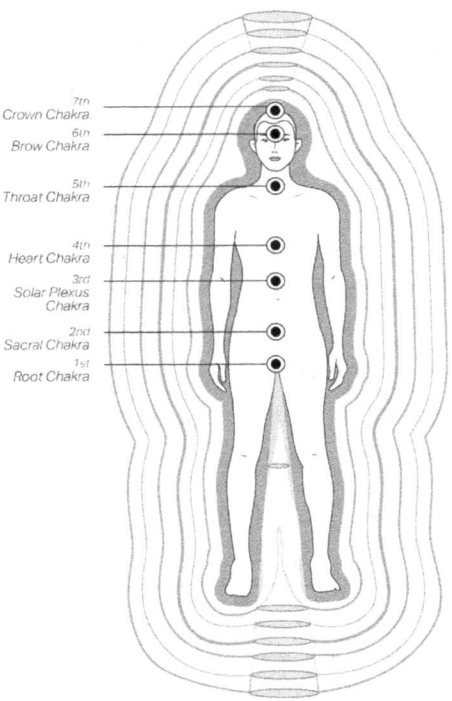

Diagram 6. Chakras

The Three Minds

The notion of the subconscious and conscious minds is well known within conventional psychology:
- The subconscious mind: the seat of instinctual beliefs, patterns and behaviours.
- The conscious mind: the seat of beliefs, patterns and behaviours we are aware of and consciously work with.

When it comes to psycho-spirituality, the notion of a third mind is necessary: this is the superconscious mind. While the subconscious mind can be mapped to the lower mental body, the superconscious mind can be mapped to the soul. The conscious mind is the bridge between the two where you can consciously clear what does not serve in the subconscious mind and feed it with supporting thoughts / images / impressions / emotions and call on the superconscious mind to guide you.

To use the metaphor of the garden: if the gardener is not tending the garden, weeds and brambles grow and take over. The work of the gardener (conscious mind) is then to clear all weeds and cut or burn the brambles (limiting beliefs, disserving patterns), and invite a higher order and beauty into the garden (superconscious mind). The conscious gardener has another role which is to access the wisdom and guidance of the superconscious mind to envision the plan for the garden and tend to it in alignment with divine will.

The Three Minds

Subconscious Mind	Conscious Mind	Superconscious Mind
Record keeper of all thoughts, impressions, memories, images, impressions, impulses, desires, habit, patterns, messages… throughout lifetimes. Categorizes, sorts, prioritises data continuously. Creates vital force. Law of Attraction. Metaphor – Garden.	Director of the personality. Sets Intention, direction and takes decisions with discipline, discernment, willpower, concentration, reasoning. Orchestrates Self. Metaphor – Gardener.	Spiritual Mind. Conveys Divine Wisdom, Intelligence, Love, Guidance… upon request. Available to be consulted through meditation, tuning-in through the subtle senses, through art, music, sound… Law of Free Will. Metaphor – Muse, Garden Spirit.

The subconscious mind is never inactive, and it stores everything you have consciously and mostly unconsciously allowed to be impressed upon it throughout all your incarnations: experiences / encounters / people and beings / places / atmospheres; sounds / music / songs / voices / melodies; images / movies / social media impressions; stories / narratives / thoughts and beliefs you have ever had; emotions you have ever felt. In the subconscious mind, the impressions on the five senses and your inner narrative create conclusions.

Whenever the conscious mind is not actively in charge, that is when you are not fully anchored in presenceness, and the subconscious mind takes over. A conscious effort is required to surrender the subconscious mind to the conscious mind, and then the conscious mind to the superconscious mind.

The Two Levels of Parenting and the Soul-Monadic Structure

Parenting through the eyes of Source is anchored in the spiritual aspects of Self. We have called this earlier in this book, the soul. It is a fundamental difference to conventional parenting and for this reason, we wish to shed clarity on some of the terms we will be using in this book. For simplicity, we will distinguish between two levels of parentings which we will call in this book:
- The Soul Level.
- The Personality Level.

However, it is important that we explain what both entails. Let's start with the personality level which is where most people derive their sense of self and mean when they say "I".

Personality Level

When you think of "personality", you may associate it with a fixed constitution, but the personality is far from being fixed. Personality is a construct and as such is completely mutable. There is nothing eternal nor fixed about it. The personality is like a bucket, a container. However, changing the contents of the bucket is a conscious process: if you do not apply intention and dedication to change what is within your personality, it will remain.

Let's look at what remains exactly. For simplicity, let's imagine that you are having your very first incarnation (this is far from being the case): at this point you begin with an empty bucket. At the moment of conception, whatever experiences you are having generate impressions from which you draw conclusions and on and on with every experience that you have throughout your first lifetime. During this first incarnation, any given conclusion will remain the same unless you draw a new conclusion which replaces it. At the moment of death, all of the experiences which have filled your personality bucket with conclusions are overseen by your spiritual guidance and validated for the next incarnation. These conclusions accumulate and energetically they reside within the divine light structure that you are. In other words, electrons within your divine light structure become charged with these conclusions. Remember that you have free will, so no-one but yourself can remove or change the conclusions you have made.

Now you arrive in your second incarnation and your personality energetic grids are not empty but already charged with all the conclusions of your first lifetime. And it goes on. Every time you upgrade a conclusion, it will change: if you don't, it will remain in the bucket. More conclusions can be added, but no conclusion is removed unless you consciously work with them. Every human being on Earth now has had on average 280 lifetimes already (many have had many more). Stereotypes, biases, personality tests and profiling are all tapping into the personality bucket as if it were a constant. But if you began working with your conclusions, you would see that your personality would shift.

Even what we call "character" (for example, jovial or taciturn) is the emotional expression of the conclusions you have carried throughout multiple incarnations and not changed. When the conclusions are made and added to the 'bucket' they were deemed by your personality - soul extension - to be useful, and they were. But this is not always the case in your new incarnation. This is what then causes limitations.

The structure of universal vibration makes it so that our vibrational frequency - and in this case we mean the vibrational frequency of our personality (soul extension) - informs our lived experience. Therefore, if we gather a conclusion during a lived experience where our vibration is low, our conclusions will contain the same vibration. This means that as we take our spiritual journey in other lives, our vibration is impacted by the conclusions which are in our bucket. As we go on and have new experiences, we may increase our vibration and thus shift our conclusions (both the content and vibration of them).

When old conclusions do not sit well with new conclusions or some of our conclusions are of different vibrations, we experience an inner conflict or discomfort. Some of the conclusions are not blocking us, but others are. Some may even be irrelevant to the current life we are experiencing, but because they have not been examined and cleared from the personality bucket, they are still active within us. For example, if you had multiple lives in which you drew out of your lived experiences a conclusion of "needing to be obedient", this conclusion may no longer be helpful in your current life. If that's the case, if it sits unexamined in your personality bucket, it is impacting your reality and personal power. In this case, it would serve you to revisit and amend it.

So, through our spiritual journey we have gathered various sets of conclusions which have been informed by our 'relative to that life' lived experiences. At some point, we revisit these conclusions to see which ones are no longer resonating with our present vibration. We may then choose to transmute or transform these conclusions so they can no longer inform our present lifetime experience - and no longer limit, colour or inhibit our present experience. This is often referred to as clearing the four lower bodies.

For the sake of clarity, simplicity and to use common language, which is also workable, when we talk about the personality level in this book, we mean the four lower bodies from the comprehensive view we detailed earlier:
- The physical
- The etheric
- The emotional
- The lower mental (the subconscious mind)

Conventionally, when you say "I" you are referring to this level. In sourceness and parenting as a Light path described in this book, we are only interested in the personality level for two purposes:
- That it is healthy, balanced and ideally nourished with firm unconditional love.
- That it is in a state of surrenderedness to the soul level and it occupies its ideal place as the Garden instead of the Gardener.

When you say "I" from the soul level, you are recognizing your inherent sourceness and refer to the oversoul which we will describe in the next section.

Soul Level

The soul level refers to the spiritual bodies described earlier in the comprehensive view of the human body system. At the soul level, there is an individual and a collective aspect. We feel that in recent years, the word 'soul' which has been widely popularised is used with great confusion and mostly refers to the soul extension level rather than what it actually implies. Let's clarify this here.

The individual "soul" is called a soul extension, and this is composed of four lower bodies or the personality level we just described. However, what we traditionally call "a soul" is an oversoul which is composed of 12 soul extensions. This is the collective aspect and that is what soul is: a group of individual soul extensions. It is a bit like the garlic knob which is made of multiple cloves.

The inherent nature of "soul" is that of one-ness. The personality which sees itself as standalone cannot experience that. Even if your conscious mind has a rational understanding that everything in this world is interconnected, it cannot have the experience of one-ness. The oversoul has that experience and your basis of operation becomes the oversoul once you have soul merged, meaning the personality is to a wide extent surrendered to the oversoul. A complete soul merge is when the 12 soul extensions of one oversoul have completely integrated the oversoul and at this stage, there is not much personality left at all.

Integrating the oversoul is a fundamental spiritual stage of initiation for the individual soul extension. To reach this, the oversoul can be contacted for guidance and support on the challenges you face in your life and your integration process. This is what we mean when we say that you may contact your team in Spirit for assistance and guidance (please read the dedicated section on this). Please understand that it is your job to work towards this initiation and nobody else's. This begins with the realisation that you are the oversoul and not personality only. The spiritual landscape continues after the oversoul: there are an infinite number of levels you can 'progress' on.

The monad is the next level of collective grouping and is composed of 12 oversouls. In your monad, you as the soul extension are one of 144 soul extensions. Your divine blueprint is defined at the monadic level, and this is your eternal spark of sourceness.

For simplicity and clarity purposes, when we talk about the soul level in this book, we mean the oversoul. But you can see that, 'soul' refers to all the levels beyond oversoul and it depends where you are at in each divine now moment. The further you develop and integrate, the greater the range of soul levels you work with. But let's leave this for now and focus here on the oversoul as the soul level.

The major difference that we wish to distinguish between what we call the personality level, and the soul level is the conscious connection to the Divine. Beginning to see yourself as a soul extension on an evolutionary journey towards an oversoul and a monadic integration is a fundamental shift we invite you to consider.

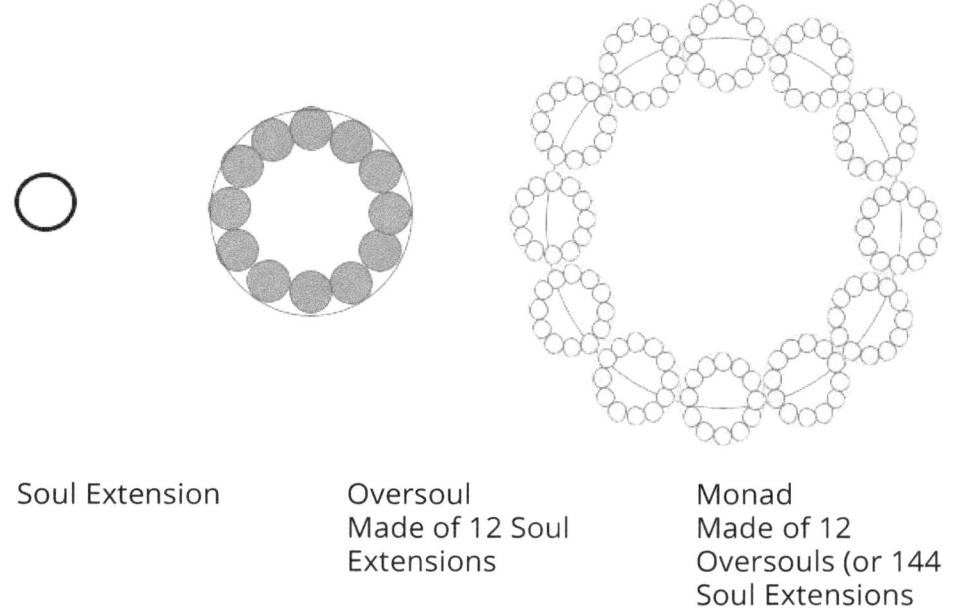

| Soul Extension | Oversoul
Made of 12 Soul
Extensions | Monad
Made of 12
Oversouls (or 144
Soul Extensions |

Diagram 7. The Soul - Monadic Structure

For your understanding of the spiritual landscape, we have included below the further stages of evolution/integration until the Cosmic Monad in a simplified way (see Diagram 8. The Cosmic Monadic Structure).

The purpose of spiritual evolution, for each spiritual body is to grow and integrate into the next level. So, if you are operating as the soul extension, the next stage is the oversoul; if you are operating at the oversoul level, the next stage is the monad.

At each level, there is one soul extension who has contracted for the others the responsibility of integration of the entire structure. At the oversoul level, there is one soul extension who has the responsibility of integrating all the other 11. At the monadic level, there is one soul extension who has the responsibility to integrate all the other 143 soul extensions of the monad, and so on.

The further you go, the more collective the work of integration. Also, the process of growth and integration is not linear: it is likely that you work in parallel on multiple levels.

We are not expecting that you make sense of all this information here, especially if you are reading about it for the first time. Full understanding is not the purpose of this book. However, it will come in handy at a later stage. For now, please know that there is tremendous order in the universe and there is indeed a Divine Plan for all of us on the Path of Light. The spiritual growth and integration one achieves in a given incarnation is determined in one's divine blueprint - this is completely individual. In this sense there is no standard path, and all paths are ideal.

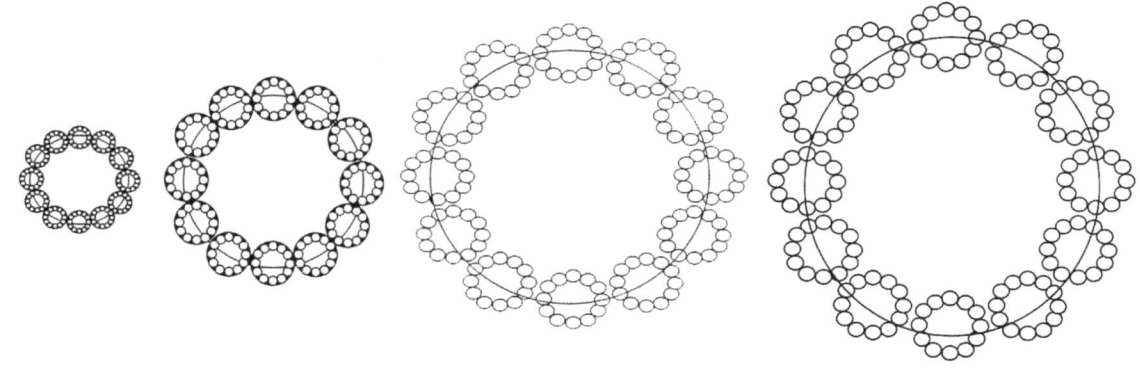

| Monad | Group Monad
Made of 1'728
Soul Extensions
or 12 Monads | Planetary Level
Monad
Made of 20'736
Soul Extensions | Cosmic Level
Monad
Made of 248'832
Soul Extensions |

Diagram 8. The Cosmic Monadic Structure

The more integration we have of each monadic body, the more light, wisdom, unconditional love, divine power, harmony and joy we are and radiate all around. One of the principles of this book is to invite parents to shift their basis of operation from personality only to soul level and see their children as oversouls on an evolutionary journey. When we talk about "soul to soul" parenting, what we mean here is oversoul to oversoul. This is important because many children are currently incarnated with a partial soul merge.

Our Spark of Source Energy

"The Source is a fine, pure energy that we have been given a spark of, and the spark that we have been given is at the monadic level. The monadic level extends into a format of a stream of energy which contains points of realisation, one of which has been called the Oversoul and one of which has been called your physical expression (physical body and personality self)." [iv]

Parenting – Book One

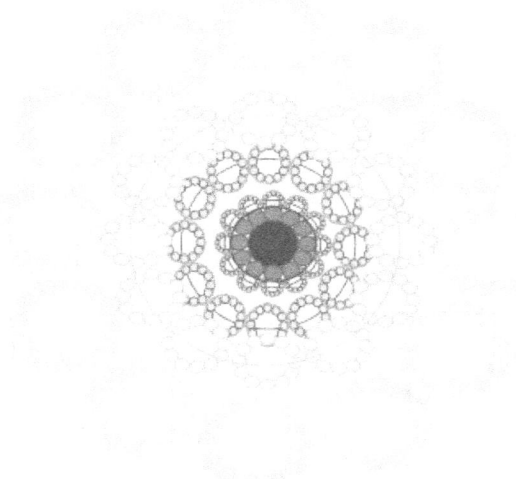

Diagram 9. Integrated Soul Extension into Cosmic Monad

More About Monadic Structures

There are infinite numbers of monads, each following the structure described. God created infinite numbers of monads, and each monad then created twelve souls/oversouls so that it could experience a denser form of matter than previously experienced. Each soul/oversoul then created 12 personalities or soul extensions. Not all soul extensions within an oversoul are in a physical incarnation, not all are on Earth. Djwhal Khul, Master of Wisdom, Wisdom Council of Earth has said there are 60,000 million monads working through our earthly planetary system. Multiplying 60,000 million by 144 we have the number of soul extensions/personalities involved in the process of reincarnation on this planet = 60,000,000,000 times 144 = 8,640,000,000,000. The current world population is 8,117,344,536 and increasing as of 21/06/2024 meaning that there are soul extensions working on the earthly plane who are not physically incarnated!

A Word About the Incarnation Process and the Soul Merge

Physical conception of a child begins when the female egg is fertilised by a spermatozoid. In this moment, the soul begins its journey into incarnation and a link is made between the physical embryo and the monad. That link will remain throughout the lifetime of the child until death. However, the spiritual aspect of self does not anchor in the body until a process called the soul merge which is when the personality is fully integrated into the oversoul. The soul merge is not an automatic process. For some people, this requires their conscious effort and spiritual commitment. For some, and this is oftentimes the case of children currently being incarnated on Earth, they already come to life with its partial integration. The soul merge is a fundamental step of spiritual evolution: at this stage, the oversoul is the primary reference for the conscious mind.

A complete soul merge means that sovereignty of the individual is with the spiritual aspect of self and not the physical (physical body / personality) and when the integration is complete, the individual is no longer the object of his/her psychological fluctuations. This means that when the soul merge is complete, at the personality level, the individual's mind is calm, the emotions stable and peaceful and this, regardless of outer conditions.

What is the Soul Merge?

The soul merge is an outcome of the process of spiritual growth or ascension/descension. Soul merge is when your mastery of your physical body, emotional/astral body and mental body (all at the personality level) allows your soul/oversoul to merge with your physical body.

The soul merge is when your oversoul becomes the 'guide of your physical ship,' so it may begin to guide your personality on the mission to realise the oversoul blueprint. Your oversoul has a higher consciousness than your personality/soul extension. Your oversoul can provide clear guidance because it 'knows' (has access to, understands, interprets, etc.) the blueprint. The Soul Blueprint is the plan you made before you incarnated. Before the soul merge happens, you will have developed a beginning level of mastery over your densest body - the physical body, its appetites, requirements, sexual urges, sleep habits and so on, in service of your oversoul.

You will also have developed mastery over the second densest body which is the emotional/astral body and its emotional surges and desires to a certain degree in service of the oversoul. Conscious intent and continual choice-making to develop your mastery are what is required here. Material desires are beginning to be transformed into spiritual desire for liberation and freedom. You have learned to avoid being a victim of your desires and emotions, and instead to be a master and cause.

The vast majority of what is written and conveyed today on human development, leadership and parenting is established from the personality level and addresses the personality level. Consequently, our current human systems - social, political, economic, educational - are stemming from the personality view. This is a major gap and limits our human potential, dismissing aspects currently necessary to help us change and welcome the next stage of our and Earth's evolution.

This is why the soul level is foundational in this book: in order to access the tools which, support our evolution, we need to shift our basis of operation from focus on personality only to include our soul level and also begin practices that help us anchor in unconditional love, higher wisdom and divine power, which are in our soul level.

A key question to ask yourself is: "Is it in my current incarnation divine blueprint to soul merge?" Allow the answer to come to you from your oversoul - do not allow the personality to give the answer. You can ask this question many times and allow the time needed to receive a clear answer. To know from within you what the answer is.

Look for the answer inside your question. Rûmi

Your Central Channel: The Antahkarana Bridge

We make a clear distinction throughout the book, and for the purpose of simplicity, between the personality and the soul levels of parenting. When the personality level is surrendered and integrated into the soul level, our humanity is complete, and we can function as we have been meant to function as a whole divine being having an earthly physical experience with the bodies/minds that enable the realisation and enjoyment of this experience. This process, as we have explained, requires the conscious decision and effort of everyone: until this process is complete, you are still (to a wider or lesser degree) led by the personality and experience yourself as a separate individual disconnected from Source. It may also be worthwhile mentioning that we do not, at time of publication, know anyone incarnated on Earth who has no personality level in them - this calls for continuous humility and self-examination but also offers relief that there is complete imperfection in our perfect path.

The process of spiritualisation involves the conscious animation of the spiritual link between the personality and the oversoul which is called the Antahkarana bridge or central channel. For most adults at this time, this bridge still needs to be consciously animated, which is not the case for many of the children currently incarnated who seem to have come with an existing pre-animated Antahkarana bridge - at least it is more advanced in its development than many adults have.

There is an effective process to build the central channel and ideally adjust its size. You can find this process in the *Sourceness Journal*. You will also find multiple additional exercises once you have built your central channel to further build and reinforce your connection to oversoul and Source. This is the very first step in your spiritual journey and it marks your conscious decision to lead an oversoul led life.

Sourceness: A Series for Golden Earth Being

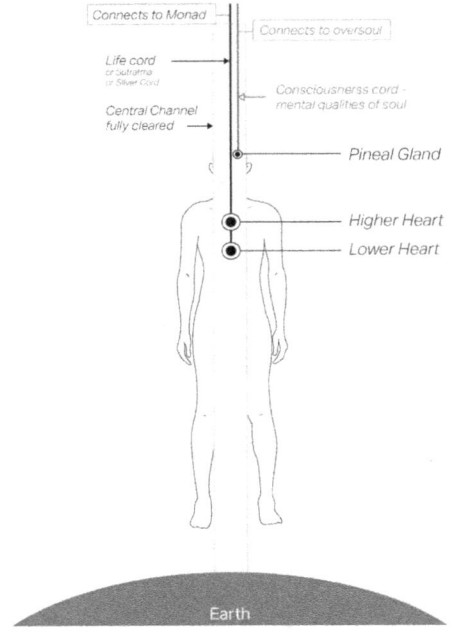

Diagram 10. The Antahkarana Bridge 1

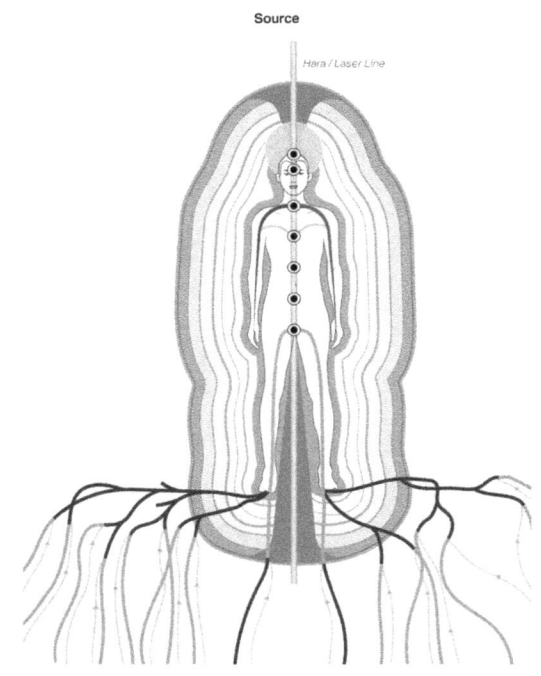

Diagram 11. The Antahkarana Bridge - Part 2

Chapter 2
The Parent Light Path and Practice

Parenting as a Light Path

Among all the experiences on your spiritual journey of incarnation some are pleasant and agreeable while others are uncomfortable and painful; however, all are part of the experience, and all are your soul level decision. All beings who are on a Path of Light, and that includes you and everyone you know, no matter how distant they may seem from it in any given period of their lives, belong to the Light, are of Light.

As you have chosen to be a Parent, your spiritual path is intertwined with parenting. This may also be the case even if you don't become a parent yourself - for example people who have a chosen profession of teacher, caregiver, child therapist or child counsellor, are also likely to have a soul mission of working with children. The parenting Light Path, just like any other Soul Path involves several initiations which are like milestones on your journey, very much like degrees you would get from school. However, unlike degrees, there is no story attached to "passing or failing the test" - no judgement, no comparison. There is also no ranking, for everyone on a light path has already succeeded, although this may not yet be in your conscious awareness.

Initiations are gateways and map the path in a structured way which makes it digestible for us. They tell you how well you have mastered a certain set of challenges relative to each initiation and soul mastery requires you to continuously keep up with the requirements of each gateway. As mentioned, there is no expiry date, and you cannot fail: you really have eternity to succeed. However, once you consciously embark on this journey, you also realise how deeply motivating, inherently satisfying and enriching it is. You realise step by step that all your suffering are self-imposed limitations and strive to delimit yourself: on that path, there is no enemy, everyone belongs, is worthy by the nature of being a divine oversoul, can reclaim one's divine sovereignty, radiate unconditional love, divine wisdom and power and will receive all the support one asks.

A Word on Spiritual Initiations

What we mean by initiations has nothing to do with religious rituals that create a sense of belonging or acceptance. Initiations are more like the grading system at school where you pass the first grade and move on to the next grade after meeting a certain number of requirements to pass the level.

The difference, however, is that "the degree" (used here as a metaphor because there really is not any degree) is not given to you by someone other than yourself. This is why honesty and discernment are a critical mindset and commitment for everyone who takes this path seriously. Guidance and confirmation from ascended masters, guides and teachers is available to all who take this path. These masters, guides and teachers who have taken responsibility to care for others while also progressing further on their own paths.

There cannot be any space for ego aggrandisement (being at a "higher spiritual grade" than you are) or deflation (being at "a lower grade than you"). This also means that you will need to make the decision to step away from looking and searching outside to Teachers, Masters and Gurus to lay the path for you and instead call on your superconscious mind and team in Spirit to guide you from within. Your team in Spirit / guides act like your inner teachers and they can provide guidance on the challenges you are facing, the learnings you are aiming to master, the support you need... The spiritual path is like a school where your entire team is holding your highest well-being into account and with encouragement and support looks forward to seeing you complete each grade or initiation.

Each initiation corresponds to a set of skills, attitudes, learnings, mindsets and is complete when you have fully integrated it. For example, to return to the example of the three minds, one of the initiations is the mastery over the subconscious mind: this mastery means that in every divine now moment, you have full clarity over what is going on in your subconscious mind and have it surrendered to your oversoul. Another initiation is to operate in every divine now moment through the eyes of unconditional love vs. fear. As you can appreciate all these initiations are serving your full integration as an oversoul into the divine being you are.

As a parent you are also an adult, and this has implications on your Light Path - You are acting as a Guide to the children for whom you accepted responsibility. Your spiritual path involves not only yourself but also that of your children until they are of age of taking care of themselves - nominally 16-18 years of age:

- This will likely involve specific challenges which are at the intersection of your over soul's journey.
- It also means that your personal work is at the forefront of your parenting. To your child, you are the safe harbour, the lighthouse, the sandy beach, the meadow, the anchor, the clearing storm... all together, depending on what the divine now moment requires of you. This will require pliancy and flexibility from you.
- This will also require that you spend dedicated time to tune into what is going on for your child beyond the outer manifestation you experience. For example, to bring harmony for her until she can do this herself when she is out of balance or to get the messages of his oversoul to understand what is going on for him.

- This also involves the clearing of "weeds and brambles" from your child's subconscious mind.

As parents, your "work" often lies just in front of you, in what your children play out for you. Every parent can relate to how challenging some situations with their kids are: the children's dramas of frustration and anger, their refusals and rejections... They call you in, testing all your buttons. It takes fortitude in the conscious mind to step on the balcony and detach yourself from these heated situations which are directly tapping into your own subconscious mind's programs and draw your emotional body into fear: anger, hopelessness, despair, resentment... But what if your children's dramas were the exact gift that you need to explore the deepest confines of your own suppressed, forgotten, overlooked subconscious mind or emotional body? In the presence of pure unshakable unconditional love, no drama can find the fuel it needs for its fire. If there is no limiting program within you, there is no button to be pushed. If you are reacting or are even the slightest bit disturbed, there is an invitation for you to look within your personality (four lower bodies): find the dissonant thread, infuse it with love and forgiveness, heal it, clear it and transmute it. This is the path of mastery that we are invited to take.

It is also useful to say that this is a very **joyful path** and the garden that awaits you once you have removed the obstruction of the overgrown weeds will warm your heart in a way where you will experience a sense of homecoming and deep relief, peace and joy. This is the reward of the spiritual path. We experience it and move on.

A Word About 'Points of Realisation'

"...there are initiations, if you wish to call them that—we could call them points of realisation—available on the physical level, and the beginning of understanding beyond that point, which will show that the divine process has developed a great deal through physical existence.

A point of realisation is where contact, when energised, brings an alignment of the four-body system with divine flow. Physical, emotional, mental and spiritual concepts, understandings and structures align which gives a greater rate of divine flow than before that realisation occurred." [v]

Navigating in Your Own Rhythm

While with gardening there seems to be such a thing as beginner and advanced, on the spiritual Path there is no such comparison because it is far more complex than that. For the sake of making it easier to navigate, we will use the same analogy, mostly because some tools have to be mastered first before others can be introduced. For example, if you have not built your central channel (we will introduce this later in the book), you cannot do practices which involve it. The building of your central channel simply has to come first; and if you don't know what your central channel is, then you need to start there.

In the *Sourceness Journal* section, exercises and practices which are offered take this into account and you can identify which "level" best suits your readiness and needs at that moment. As such, there is no beginner's or advanced practice, and we encourage you to drop this polarity. This is due to a widespread belief in our humanity that there are teachers and those who learn from them - especially on the Spiritual Path, many traditions have considered (and still do) that one - needs to be initiated by another human who is granted the Master role. Please read the box "Message from Source on The Path of Light" below for further input on this. As we have mentioned earlier, the spiritual path is one of turning within and becoming your own Gardener, rather than looking outside for guidance. This will likely involve a process of healing, clearing, weeding and transformation for yourself.

This book applies to all beings and there will be something in it for everyone who seeks to parent from their oversoul. However, if anything feels completely out of balance with you and feels against your truth in the divine moment you are reading it, please do use your **free will to choose what is true to you.** Some things will not resonate because they are so far away from where mass consciousness is today, so we do not invite you to read this book from your lower mind; instead tune into yourself/oversoul to go beyond the limitations of the sub-conscious mind, the fears and hurts which you genuinely suspect are in the way.

A Word About Truth

"Truth is as variable as all of the beings who seek it. Your truth is not necessarily the same as someone else's truth. It is not meant to be, because total truth is made up of all the opinions of everyone that exists.

Truth is the totality of the expressions in which each one sees a little differently and in which each person has a complementary point of view that feeds into the whole point of view and that allows it to be an unlimited expression therein.

There are many, many ways to view everything." [vi]

Our intention is to enable parents to eventually use all these tools by themselves and directly speak with their spiritual Guides; yet you may experience a learning gap or discomfort as you begin this journey, and some things may feel like a stretch - there is no judgement involved here. The spiritual journey involves stretches. For example, in the beginning and to borrow once more the metaphor of the Garden, it is likely that gardening will begin by clearing your limiting beliefs and programs, healing your wounds and removing dense energies from your body system. It is understandable that you will seek support in the face of the amount and depth of weeds and brambles to address and possibly some of the walls in the garden are crumbling under the weight of vegetation gone wild and you will require an upgrade of your inner energetic "walls" - until you can do it by yourself. We are not discouraging support, on the very contrary.

You are the one to decide when and if and how you seek help. You are the Gardener. This book offers guidance and tools that will help you take ownership of your Path. It will help you develop greater understanding of who you are and offer you bridges to the various aspects of Self. Ultimately, you are the one deciding what to use or not.

We would like to stress here that accessing your subtle senses, communicating with your team in Spirit and superconscious Mind, developing your self-healing abilities, remembering who you are as the oversoul and what you have come to be on this planet are available to all and not limited in any way. It is within the reach of every human being to:
- develop their clairvoyant / clairsentient / clairaudient / 'clair'-knowing skills.
- to receive the direct guidance of their soul and team in Spirit.
- to channel information and messages from the ascended masters.
- to self-heal and live harmoniously within themselves and their environment.
- to remember the purpose of their soul journey in this incarnation.
- to be of service to their sourceness.

For many years we have believed that spiritual realisation is a holy aspiration of which we can at best, get a distant fragrance on our deathbed if we have worked hard throughout our entire lifetime with the hope of a reward in an afterlife. We are very honoured to share with you here that this is a myth which no longer applies. Spiritual realisation is the essence of life, the purpose of our incarnation and it has no end. In a way, it is the beginning of your divine journey.

Message from Source on The Path of Light

You are on a Path of Light for this is the purpose of your soul journey.
It does not matter how far you believe you have fallen off track, you still are on the Path.
I, as the I AM Presence, the I AM That I AM, call you back to that.
It is by recognizing your own I AM Presence that you return to that which you call home.
When you say the Soul Mantra or the Monadic Mantra, you experience that which you are immutably: I AM THAT I AM, I am ALL, I AM Light. LIGHT, LIGHT, LIGHT.
Your Path of Light, which is unique to each one of you dear soul is to reclaim your pure Light essence. I experience Myself through you, as the Light and I expand through you as the Light. There is no You or I when there is Light experiencing itself as Light.
Our journey into, through, within, from... the Light evolves as we, the One, recognize that we are the Light and consciously accept this Light. There is no we, there is just Light experiencing itself as Light.
Not becoming Light. Not returning to the Light. Not growing into the Light or embracing or embodying more Light. No: Being all the Light that you already are. Now and into eternity and infinity. In this Now and every Now.
You are on the Path. Realise it.

Creating a Meditation Practice - Observation, Reflection & Silence

We will use the practice of meditation in various forms throughout the book and in the *Sourceness Journal*. To make it convenient for you, we have recorded these meditations, and you can find them on the www.sourceness.one website.

Meditation has become very popular in recent years, and we would like to clarify what we mean by meditation. **Meditation** is a practice of stilling yourself and tuning in to observe what is from your inner balcony as well as access your superconscious mind. Stillness is necessary to watch carefully and with discernment: if you place your gaze on a wild garden where plants grow in all directions, it will take attention and clarity of mind to spot the specific plant you are looking for, especially if there is wind or rain. To some extent and for most of us, our inner garden has not been tended before we start our conscious spiritual work: plants have grown wild, strong weeds have covered the ground and overshadow the flowers which no longer have the space they need and the walking paths to navigate are no longer visible. Over time, you may even forget that there is a beautiful flower under all the brambles and not notice it anymore.

Some of the meditation practises in this book involve **visualisations.** Visualisations feed the subconscious mind and when they are used with clear intent, they can reprogram it for your highest well-being. The visualisations we will use aim at lighting up the garden path hidden under the weeds, highlighting some stepping stones and/or creating new ones to enable you to navigate your garden as you clear it, nourish and cultivate it anew. As you practise visualisation, you will begin the process of remembering dimensions and aspects which are buried within you, forgotten or suppressed and you will experience the clear distinction between mental imagery and genuine insight.

The spiritual path we are proposing in this book is one of **self-discovery and inner mastery.** Your inner experience is the master and spiritual discernment is an important inner muscle to build and continue building in every Divine Now moment. The practice of meditation will help you build the muscle of spiritual discernment so you may, for example, distinguish if a voice alive in you is coming from your subconscious/lower mind or your oversoul.

In addition to the meditations and visualisations in the *Sourceness Journal,* we strongly encourage you to create a dedicated space for a personal **daily meditation practice.** This can take various forms and in particular, concentration meditation, observation and intuitive meditation.

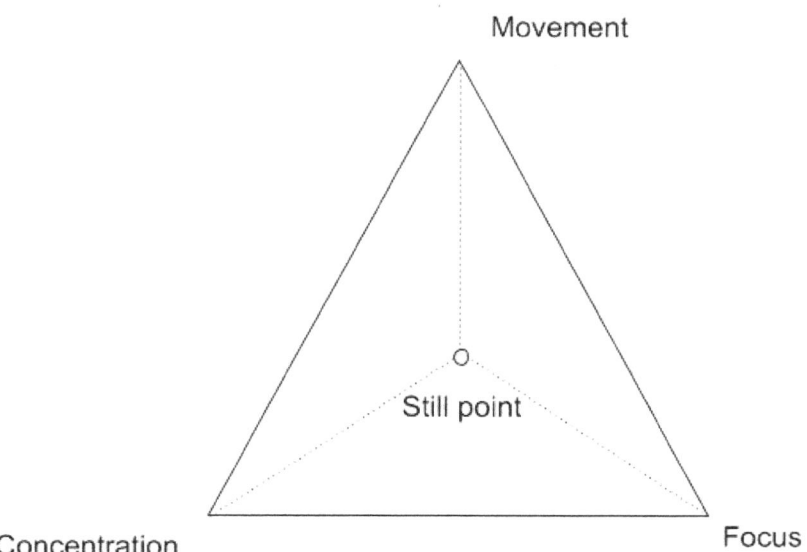

Concentration Meditation

Concentration Meditation will help you become aware of what is going on in your lower body system: physical sensations, emotions, thoughts, ideas, impressions… This is a fundamental muscle to build to be able to spot your triggers and inner dynamics as they arise. Concentration meditation is often described as a practice to calm the monkey mind. The monkey mind refers to the subconscious mind which when untamed, runs wild and does what it wants in your garden. When we talk about concentration meditation, we mean not only your subconscious mind but also your physical and emotional bodies.

For example, a certain place may have an impact on your mood; the tone of someone's voice may trigger a chain of automatic thoughts in your lower mind which in turn generate a set of emotions; a certain activity or lack of activity may have an impact in your state of mind.

You can train this muscle by practising the classical exercises described for mind training such as focusing on the breath and returning your attention to the breath every time you get distracted (by a body sensation such as itching, a noise you hear, a thought or an emotion). Then you can in time expand your practice from focusing on the breath to focusing on the entirety of your inner experience and spot what has triggered the inner experience. For example: there was a thought and as you gave your attention to it, your stomach tightened, and the emotion of fear arose. You want to be as detached as possible and as precise as possible while fully objective. There are also plenty of apps available to practise concentration meditation if you prefer this tool. Concentration meditation will help you become aware and clear about all these threads within you, and this is necessary for the mastery of the four lower bodies.

Observation

There are multiple ways to observe both your inner and outer life. The observation we refer to here implies an attitude of watching without associating with being the observer and without imprinting on what you observe. We call this detached observation. This is an art which requires practice, and you will find multiple exercises in the *Sourceness Journal.* A practice of concentration meditation will help you with building the muscle of detached observation.

We consider detached observation as another foundational muscle to develop. The personality has infinite wants and desires, many of which are clearly detrimental to your well-being and growth, for example, the third scoop of ice-cream which you know is not going to support your health. However, many of these personality desires are also disguised as helpful because they generate feelgood or excitement. A simple example is the kick of dopamine you get from seeing that someone has liked your social media post or the satisfaction you get when a group of people is valuing what you have to say. Is this beneficial to your oversoul? We let you reflect upon this. When you practise detached observation, you are prompting your subconscious mind that a big change is on its way.

There is another important reason to practise detached observation: the subconscious mind oftentimes "*thinks it knows best what is 'good for you*'". It believes it is the Gardener and when you give it this power, it directs your life. When you pause and consciously say no to automatic programming, this creates a space for the oversoul to step in.

When you practise detached observation, you are signalling to your entire lower Self your intention to be surrendered to the divine. In every situation, the Divine is at play. In every human being, the breath of God is moving. Detached observation is the foundation to help us reconnect with it.

The Scientific View on Observation and Impact on Behaviour

In 1801 Physicist Thomas Young initiated the first double path experiment famously known as "double slit" showing that light can behave both as a particle and a wave, opening the field of Quantum Physics, and opening our minds to the concept of "quantum interference".

The experiment consists in projecting particles of light through a slit and onto a screen. When there is only one slit open, as one might expect, the result is a line of light appearing on the screen. When two slits are open, our expectation to see two lines of light appearing on the screen is not verified. Instead, what we see on the screen is multiple lines of light and dark of different intensities. This has been called an interference pattern.

Further experiments have shown that when the speed of light is reduced so that physicists can observe the trajectory of single photons, they do not see as one might expect that each single photon goes either through one slit or the other. Instead, an interference pattern can be observed even with one photon which seems to travel through both slits and all possible trajectories onto the screen.

Finally, when physicists added a monitor to observe the behaviour of the photon, the trajectory of the photon changed: when the photon is observed, it will seemingly pass either through one slit or the other and create no interference.

More recently, a new version of the double slit experiment was conducted introducing a second slit after light was projected through the first one. The experiment showed that although the photon was set on its single trajectory, it changed pattern and an interference appeared as the second slit was introduced even if it had already passed the slit.

- The single photon follows its straight path onto the screen when presented with only one slit.
- The single photon interferes with itself when presented with two slits to pass through, even if the second slit is introduced later.
- The path of the photon differs when it is observed, passing through one slit or the other only without creating interference.

How does this relate to parenting? If you consider that we are all energy in motion and that our oversoul/monad as a spark of the divine are particles journeying through life, it is likely that how we observe our children and how we interact with them creates an interference in their being and path. It is also highly likely that how we observe ourselves creates an interference in our own being and path.

We do not have any judgement about interference or non-interference. However, we are pointing out that the options we see and the way we observe ourselves seeing them has an influence on our path.

Reflection

Reflection is the conscious mind's way to integrate what it is learning. It's your executive leadership tool. We have included in the *Sourceness Journal* section for each chapter reflection questions to help you in this process. We encourage you to add your own and apply reflection daily and over-time with practice, in every Divine Now Moment. For example, as you question through whose eyes you are experiencing a given situation - the personality or the oversoul? - you are reflecting. The foundation of reflection is detached observation which enables reflection to be pure.

Silence

Our modern lives are packed with stimulation. Taking time off from every stimulus in your life and being in silence is another useful practice. Most artists have praised the power of silence in their creative process. We consider silence as a foundational practice on the spiritual path. It goes hand in hand with taming the four lower bodies.

Silence will not only help you in your practice of concentration meditation and detached observation, but it will also be a great ally once you have reached a base level of clarity about your inner workings and ability to click on the pause button of your automatic programs.

Silence invites the oversoul to communicate with you and as such it is the ideal tool to listen to your oversoul's guidance.

Quietness

Inside this new love, die
Your way begins on the other side.
Become the sky.
Take an axe to the prison wall.
Escape.
Walk out like someone suddenly born into colour.
Do it now.
You're covered with thick cloud.
Slide out the side. Die,
And be quiet. Quietness is the surest sign
That you have died.
Your old life was a frantic running
From silence.
The speechless full moon
comes out now.
Rumi

Prayer

People have described prayer as 'talking with God.' That is, directly addressing God with requests for help, guidance, thanks, etc.

Establishing communication and an energetic constellation with the Universe, Source, God could be considered prayer. Our personality is not alone, no personality, no being is alone. Although we may feel that we are alone physically, spiritually we are all connected, supported, loved by God/Undifferentiated Source. This connection exists even if we are unconscious of it.

We have mentioned earlier that on your spiritual journey, a team in Spirit is overlooking you. Let us say a bit more about your team here: Your team in Spirit is the consciousness guiding you and overseeing your journey in alignment with your divine blueprint. Throughout your entire spiritual journey, you are always accompanied by a team who is here to support, guide and supervise your progress. They are your divine inner teachers, guides and counsellors.

At every incarnation, you review together the learnings and settings for the next one based on what you have already learned and what you long to experience. This is a rich and collaborative process which becomes even more interesting when you learn to communicate consciously with your team in Spirit during your incarnation.

To fully and consistently access your blueprint, communication with your team in Spirit is essential. To use the analogy of school we referred to earlier, when you are in direct communication with your team in Spirit, you gain clarity about the assignments you are working on. This makes it much easier to progress on the path and complete your initiations, doesn't it?

This is why communication flow between you and your team in Spirit is important, asking for help, asking for guidance, offering gratitude for the assistance provided may all be part of your prayer practice. This is what prayer is about.

Communicating in this way relies on using your subtle senses: developing your subtle senses goes hand in hand with communication (you can read more about this in the dedicated chapter).

When you are addressing prayers to your team in Spirit, you are addressing them to Source. Prayers can be simple:

"Source (or team in Spirit) please help me."

"Dear Source (or team in Spirit) I ask for your guidance in making this decision. Please lead me to the choice that is for my oversoul's highest well-being and the well-being of all in alignment with divine will."

Prayers can be detailed:

Dear Source (or team in Spirit), I am lost and have no clear understanding of what it is to be a parent to my beloved child. Please provide me with indisputable guidance and absolute clarity that I may proceed in this moment... My child is _____ (fill in the situation/issue) and I don't know how to _____, and _____, what do I do? What do I say? What is the action I take here? What is it essential for me to know? Say? Do? Feel?

A Word About Working With Invocations

An invocation is an affirmation that we make with great intent, calling in an energy and help that is greater than our daily self.

Mantras or invocations need to be used with sincerity and deep reverence if they are to penetrate beyond the emotional body.

To voice your invocations and as part of your daily practice, we recommend that you say the soul mantra (see page 165), with intent and say it before invoking anything, such as making a prayer.

Then take three deep breaths, breathing in the highest purest light from within and without. This will relax your body to welcome what you invoke. To support you in relaxing the body, you may focus on the brain stem (medulla oblongata) and ask it to relax with your intention and breath. As you exhale, extend the relaxation to your entire physical, emotional and mental bodies. When you feel you are in 'presentness' you are ready to voice your invocations.

The Subtle Senses

The language that the oversoul and our team in Spirit use to communicate with us is that of the subtle senses. This is communication at another level. When you enter a room and get a feel of what mood is in the group, you are using your subtle senses. When you think of someone and a short time later, they call you, you are using your subtle senses.

We all have access to all subtle senses. We all can develop all subtle senses. However, what is common is that we will have a natural preference for one sense over another. That's perfectly fine and you can navigate your path using mostly one. However, over time, as you deepen your connection to your superconscious mind and develop all your subtle senses, you may find that other senses also become available to you. In practice you may also observe that you get the stream of information through one subtle sense and process / make sense of it through another.

We will work with four subtle senses in this book:
- Clairvoyance - seeing
- Clairaudience - hearing
- Clairsentience - sensing
- Claircognizance - knowing

Senses are receiving and sending streams of information. At the personality level, they are informing you about what the personality is seeing, hearing, sensing and knowing. When we talk about subtle senses, we mean the receiving and sensing of the stream of communication that comes from the soul level or what the oversoul is seeing, hearing, sensing and knowing or what your guides / team in Spirit are communicating to you. Clair refers to clarity and what this means is that the stream is clear with information from your oversoul/Source unobstructed, untainted, undistorted...

Your daily practices of meditation, detached observation, reflection and silence will help you tune into and access your subtle senses and deeper guidance from your soul.

Clairvoyance

Clairvoyance refers to the subtle sense of seeing through the eyes of the oversoul. For your conscious awareness, this happens through images, visual flashes or even movies. The content of the visual imagery or visualisation is what the oversoul is communicating to you. Some with clairvoyant sensing have vivid dreams and access their guidance while they sleep; others access it through meditation, closing their eyes and opening their inner eyes. Others see 'video' streams of images.

Clairsentience

Clairsentience is the subtle sense of feeling in your emotional or physical body the messages of your oversoul or team in Spirit. To some people these manifest as a tingling or extra-light electric shock. The sense making of what the message is about will be more strengthened as you have developed the ability to observe (with detachment) what is happening in that moment and when you have created sufficient spaciousness within you to do so with a clear and quiet mind.

Clairaudience

Clairaudience is the subtle sense of hearing the messages or your oversoul / team in Spirit. This may manifest as clear words/sentences, sounds, melody or music.

Claircognizance

Claircognizance is the subtle sense of knowing intrinsically what your oversoul / team in Spirit is communicating to you. With claircognizance, there is no reflection process as no thoughts are involved, instead it is the immediate 'A-ha'. Like other subtle senses, claircognizance requires a clear mind and body and the spaciousness within to put the automatic programs on hold, suspend judgement and be free from triggers. However, this is subtle and requires even more calmness and trust than other subtle sensing for there is no bodily sense involved, no feeling in the physical body, and the subconscious mind needs to be particularly calm for the clarity of the information to be observed.

When Sahar was pregnant with her daughter, she and her husband took a trip to Florence and were looking for the child's name. They had agreed that they would wait until the name was given to them. During the trip, they practised observation and one day as they were hiking through the countryside, the name was as if "whispered" to them both, almost at the same time. This is an example of claircognizance.

A Word of Caution on the Delusions of Subtle Senses

We highly encourage you to give priority to developing your subtle senses and working with them as it is foundational to hone the skills of discernment, communication with your oversoul and guides and progress on your spiritual path. Subtle senses are the gateway, and connector to intuition. However, this work requires vigilance on your part and diligent screening for delusions.

Without entering paralysing doubt, it is essential to apply scrutiny and honesty to ensure that "messages" you get are not the making of your four lower bodies (hopes, desires, fears…) or manipulative information sent by energies that are not working for your highest well-being in alignment with divine will, but genuine information sent to you by your oversoul/Guides.

For more on this topic, we recommend you read the chapter on Glamour, Illusion, Maya in Dr Joshua David Stone's book, *The Complete Ascension Manual.*

There are numerous exercises and practices in the *Sourceness Journal* to assist you to build your subtle sensing abilities.

Chapter 3
Universal Consciousness

Consciousness and Group Consciousness

Being conscious has so many levels and touches upon all aspects of life. In the most common use of it, we say *'becoming conscious of'* to express something which becomes visible in our awareness. For example, when you notice that you are carried away by your thoughts, you become conscious of this identification. Or when you make the link between what you eat and how your body feels after that, you become conscious of which foods suit you or not. It is a continuous process of discovery and discernment.

Consciousness is different. Consciousness is a vibration. It is the underlying intelligence and aliveness that enables you to be conscious. All beings have consciousness: humans, plants, animals, rocks and minerals as well as other beings you may be less familiar with because they are not visible to the common mass consciousness or not on Earth.

Every oversoul belongs to a different group consciousness. Your monad, as the group of 12 oversouls you are part of is also one group consciousness which is composed of the 12-subgroup consciousness of the oversouls. When we talk about your consciousness, we mean the consciousness of your monad. All the monads in the Group monad you belong to have the same group consciousness. This is why sometimes the monad is referred to as the 'spiritual family'. A group consciousness is like a scale of vibration.

There are some common expressions which say: 'evolved consciousness' or 'advanced consciousness'. We would like to stress here that these are judgemental terms and invite you to consider dropping them. All consciousness is Source. The only difference between two group consciousness is their scales of vibration. Just like in music scales, some octaves are 'higher' than others, it doesn't make any lower octave less or inferior and higher ones more and superior. All scales are music. All consciousness is Source.

This is an important consideration because it has an impact on your life: as an oversoul /monad you have an inherent ideal set of scales to vibrate on. Aligning to your group consciousness, anchoring it in your four lower bodies, operating from that level is part of the spiritual path and part of your well-being. It is highly empowering and freeing to do so. It is our intention for humanity that all oversouls access in a clear and continuous way their group consciousness, know it and embody it. And this without any judgement for any other group consciousness.

When this happens, much of the noise in your life will be gone because you will have a clear inner knowing / feeling / sensing of who you are and what purpose is to you, and you will also know who you are not and what is not part of your path. This brings tremendous clarity, alignment, relief and trust. Much of the energy wasted in giving your attention outside of your group consciousness path will be returned to you in service to what you have come to experience.

This brings another consideration: it is not because you have a particular group consciousness that you should only communicate and get along with people within your group consciousness. This also doesn't mean that you must get along with everyone. You do and can have preferences. However, the path requires that you have no attachments.

Some group consciousnesses are so far apart (like opposite ends of vast musical scale) that they are not likely to meet. Some group consciousness can learn from one another, and they are put on each other's paths. Some group consciousness who are very close to your own vibration will feel like home, while others who are very far will feel more of a stretch.

There is no judgement to hold. If you find yourself in an environment which has what feels like a dissonant vibration to yours, it may be a sign that a change is needed for you, or maybe it is an opportunity to question the inner programs which brought you into this environment. It is not that the environment is bad. It is just that it may not be of service to your path to stay there (anymore). The more clarity you have on your own group consciousness, the clearer the guidance you can receive and the decisions you can take.

Christ Consciousness

The coming of the Golden Earth and the resolution of the challenges we are facing as a humanity throughout the world in the process of transition require us to anchor within our oversouls and monads the integrated Christ Consciousness.

When we talk about conscious parenting in this book, we refer to Christ Consciousness. Christ Consciousness is a universal consciousness that governs our planet and all of Source's creation. It is a pure consciousness of Source. To be clear here, Christ Consciousness, does not refer to Christianity, Judaism nor Jesus. As we mentioned earlier, this book is not linked to any religion.

Christ Consciousness is a state of consciousness where we see the world through the heart/mind of our GOD-ness. This means suspending all judgement, staying in a state of unconditional love and always choosing to love as the divine loves over fear.

To be a conscious parent entails all the above: It is a genuine dedication to the path that is needed with continuous love and care for one's journey.

Let us unpick this statement together:
- Seeing through the heart/mind of God refers to how we see the world. As we know it, we do not see through our eyes, but through our minds and the eyes are only a projecting tool. This points us to wards our inner work: we need to work on programs and conclusions in the personality to transcend our limitations and access our oversoul to see through the heart/mind of God.
- Refrain from all judgements: all judgements are mental distortions of what is, and as such they block the view. There is no good or bad judgement, there is only clarity or lack of it. To see through the heart/mind of God you need to be judgement-less.
- Perpetual state: refers to the ongoing process in every Divine Now moment of seeing through the heart/mind of God. Perpetual refers to time as an eternal divine now moment. The mental time of past-present-future is not relevant to the soul level which is in the Now. It is in this very moment that everything happens, exists, unfolds, emerges... When you are in Christ Consciousness in a perpetual state, then all your experience is of Christ consciousness.
- Unconditional love: refers to divine love as opposed to personality-based love, which is transactional, conditional, dividing... You can read the chapter dedicated to this for further development.
- Choosing love over fear: put simply, Love and Fear are the only two emotions. Everything that takes us out of Christ consciousness is rooted in fear. Love, unconditional, is the gateway to the heart / mind of God.

Anchoring yourself in Christ Consciousness is the highest spiritual goal you can set for yourself and a tremendous gift to your children, for you are in every Divine Now Moment operating from the heart and mind of God. As you do, you radiate unconditional love through the heart, mind and being of God, acting like a beam of light and love, thus creating the highest possible vibration all around you: one of divine harmony, perfection, stability and unity.

Your intention to be aligned with Christ Consciousness alone will accelerate your psychological integration. When you commit to Christ Consciousness then every single one of your fears and limitations will surface for you to clear and disidentify with, one by one.

This is a path of genuine humility and subtle attention. It is deeply nurturing and transforming. There are truly no words to express it.

Expression of Consciousness in The Auric Levels

Consciousness is expressed differently by the personality, oversoul and monad. As we progress the shifting of our basis of operation from personality to oversoul, we shift our consciousness.

It is important to note in the table below that as one shifts in consciousness, we move from identification with the personality - I - to a group consciousness of the oversoul and then the monad - one. Inherently, our group consciousness is collective. The soul is not individual.

There is little personality involved in the oversoul and monadic levels.

Table 2 - Expressions of Consciousness

Level 1-7	Expression of Consciousness	Statement consciousness makes
7. Ketheric	Higher Concepts	One knows one is
6. Celestial	Higher Feelings	One unconditionally loves universally
5. Etheric Template	Higher Will	One wills
4. Astral	I-thou Emotions	One loves humanly
3. Higher Mental Level	Thinking	One thinks
2. Emotional Level	Personality level emotions	I feel emotionally
2. Emotional Level	Physical sensations	I feel / sense / see / hear physically
1. Physical level	Physical functioning	I exist. I am becoming.

And just to further refine about the auric levels, below is a diagram which shows additional auric levels. We are guided that this is a partial picture of the auric structure of the human energy matrix.

According to Annemiek Douw, medium and healer, in her book, *21 Layers of the Soul*, there are 41 levels of the auric field. She says that the auric layers are part of our blueprint and so can be useful to understand what is happening in these levels. For now, it is sufficient to know that there are auric levels.

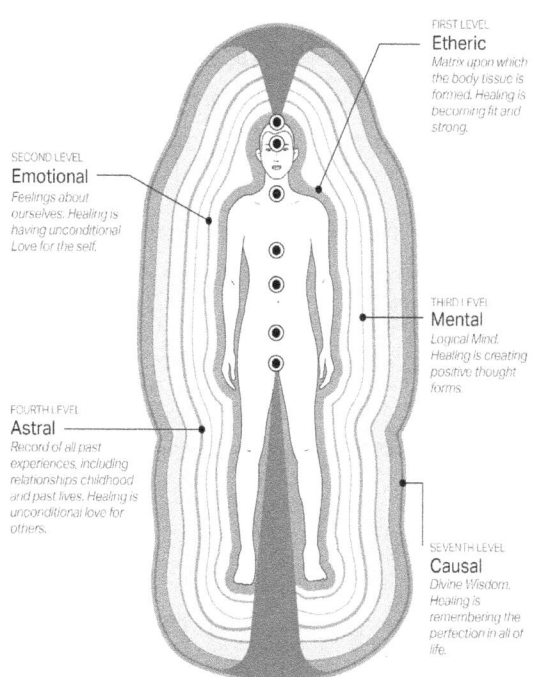

Diagram 12. Auric Levels

Your Team in Spirit and the Light Brotherhood

We have mentioned earlier about your team in Spirit:

Throughout your entire spiritual journey, you are always accompanied by a team who is here to support, guide and supervise your progress. At every incarnation, you review together the learnings and settings for the next one based on what you have already learned and what you long to experience. This is a rich and collaborative process which becomes even more interesting when you learn to communicate consciously with your team in Spirit during your incarnation.

Your team in Spirit are the guardians and stewards of your group consciousness. Your team is composed of your body elemental, oversoul, monad and guardian angel. They know exactly everything which is in alignment with divine will for you; all the agreements and contracts you have ever made; all the conclusions you have drawn; all the learnings and experiences on your spiritual path; all the programs and blockers you need to clear and every support you may need. They also know about all your progress, your priorities, the tasks you are called to accomplish within the greater divine plan and much more.

- Imagine how different your life would be if you called on your team in Spirit to:
- Ask for inputs on an experience you have
- Ask for guidance before taking a decision

- Ask for inputs on what is in alignment with divine will
- Ask for help to clear limiting beliefs/blockages and restore harmony
- Ask for assistance to heal wounds and restore health
- Ask for protection and shielding
- And so much more.

Connecting to your team in Spirit is like having your sounding board of love, wisdom and power always available to you. As we mentioned, this is not a privilege reserved to a few. Every human being can develop this ability if they so will.

Your assigned guardian angel is available to provide you comfort and is particularly keen on embracing you in its light and bathe you in unconditional love as you request it. It is here to show you the way and you can seek its assistance. If you are unsure which path is for you, you can ask your guardian angel.

Your team in Spirit is also connected to the wider universal team of the Light brotherhood. The Light brotherhood is a community of beings who are dedicated to Source as Light and to their own spiritual path. They have taken on the mission of supporting all soul extensions on their spiritual journey. These beings are much further than us on the initiation path and can therefore assist us with great wisdom and spiritual tools and light technology we can only begin to imagine. They are very keen on doing so as we request it. Some of these beings are experts in dedicated fields - such as healing or light structures. Your team in Spirit is in communication with them and as you ask for guidance, they may point you towards some of them.

The Body Elemental

Since the day Source formed/brought into being your divine spark/oversoul, the very first individuated aspect of your being, and breathed life into this aspect, you were assigned a body elemental as your unseen bodyguard and personal physician. Your body elemental is unique to your group consciousness.

This devoted consciousness has been your constant companion throughout all your incarnations. The body elemental oversees manifesting the divine blueprint in any given incarnation. Innocent and childlike, masterful and intelligent, your body elemental often appears as approximately three feet tall—almost an exact replica of you.

If you are operating at the soul extension level and working your way towards oversoul integration, your body elemental is likely to look like your soul extension. Further on the path, when you have integrated the oversoul and are working your way towards integrating the monad, your body elemental will likely look like your oversoul...

You address the body elemental in different ways depending on where you are on your path. For now, we have said that this book is about integrating the oversoul and therefore this is how to address the body elemental: body elemental of "state your name" as the soul extension you are.

Your Body Elemental takes its cues from you

Your body elemental takes its cues from you. It is a mimic of your moods and mandates. Whether you say, "I am well" or "I am sick," "I feel good" or "I feel bad," the body elemental will carry out your wish. That is why all the advice you hear about having a "positive mental attitude" is true. Whether or not you acknowledge the existence of your body elemental, your body elemental takes its orders from you and acts according to your will. All your thoughts and feelings are transferred to it, and it immediately programs them into the cells of your body. It does not matter to the body elemental if your thoughts are conscious or unconscious, it will attend to all of them.

If you train your body elemental to think negatively, by thinking negative thoughts, it will obey. Watch carefully the limitations you impose on yourself. For example, if you decide you must have so many hours of sleep, you can eat only certain foods, you can only do a specific type of work, you will catch a cold if you are in a draft, etc., your body elemental will take these as instructions.

These concepts become accepted by your subconscious mind and affect you more than you may realise. They may be out pictured by your body elemental, which thinks it is obeying your wishes. If you feel sick, if you have concepts of chronic conditions, the body elemental begins to bear the weight of that consciousness and may even begin to stoop over. Some body elementals appear hunchbacked because they are so weighted down by people's fears about their bodies.

Doubts and fears can paralyse your body elemental—many have such great fears that they completely deprive their body elemental of the opportunity to do its perfect work of healing and caring for the body. A positive attitude toward life can help it establish health and well-being.

Your body elemental has knowledge of the workings of the body that is far beyond the attainment of medical science today. Appeal to your body elemental to heal your body, it will obey. The results, of course, depend on your state of mind and attitude as well as your willingness to follow a health regimen that suits your specific needs. As part of your mastery of healing, think about building a working relationship with your body elemental.

You can of course, as a parent, also work with your child's body elemental. Before working with your child's body elemental, we recommend that you complete the clearing and healing of your own body elemental using the process that is contained in the *Sourceness Journal*.

We have also included exercises in the *Sourceness Journal* to help you curb subconscious disempowering thoughts which do not serve you.

Body Intelligence

Your intelligence is always with you,
overseeing your body, even though
You may not be aware of its work.
If you start doing something against
Your health, your intelligence
Will eventually scold you.
If it hadn't been so lovingly close by,
And so constantly monitoring,
how could it rebuke?
You and your intelligence
Are like the beauty and the precision
Of an astrolabe.
Together, you calculate how near
Existence is to the sun!
Rumi

The Spiritual Hierarchy and the Mahatma

In addition to your team in Spirit, there are many other consciousnesses and light beings who can be called upon for guidance and assistance. These are usually highly initiated beings who are the Light and devoted to the Light. We have referred earlier to the Light Brotherhood. These beings belong to what is called the spiritual hierarchy.

The Spiritual Hierarchy

The Spiritual Hierarchy functions as the Spiritual Government. It is not a government like those in any country on Earth. The Spiritual Hierarchy functions in a hierarchical structure. There is no competition between levels of the hierarchy - there is only a shared intention and mission to serve the divine in ever-expanding unity and oneness with the whole.

For further detailed information about the form and nature of the Spiritual Hierarchy we direct you to Chapter 2 of Joshua David Stone's book, *A Beginner's Guide to the Path of Ascension.* Here you will find a complete explanation of what is meant by the Spiritual Hierarchy.

The Mahatma

The request to prepare this book has initially come to us through the guidance of the Mahatma. The Mahatma is made available to us to progress and accelerate our path for the coming of Golden Earth. Mahatma, also called the Avatar of Synthesis, is a cosmic being (we are not talking about Mahatma Gandhi) that embodies 352 levels of initiations and levels all the way from Undifferentiated Source (The Creator, All That Is) to Earth.

It is a very precious gift to us that this energy is here to support each one of us who requests it and that we can communicate with it while we are in our physical bodies. Mahatma is integrated light in its purest form that we can call upon to help us do our own clearing and integration work. To help put things into perspective, Jesus when he was physically incarnated on Earth in the lifetime that we all know was completing his fifth initiation. Our personality level is really a very small part of the comprehensive energy formatting of our Being (but nonetheless essential for our earthly experience).

Mahatma, like all beings of the Spiritual Hierarchy, is an energy and a consciousness… This energy is available to all of us as we invoke it and ask it to work with us. It is particularly helpful for integration, that is integrating energy, beliefs, thoughts, emotions… and progressing towards the soul merge.

Chapter 4
Conscious Parenting

You may already know that you cannot change the world nor change others, but only yourself. All of the reality we experience is a construct of our mind. This is an important point to reflect on for parents and generally for all adults: everything which we experience in life or in relationship with other people and every situation is happening within us. We really understand this when we begin to operate at the oversoul level and beyond, when we realise that we are collective by nature.

Conscious parenting is about fully taking responsibility for oneself and everything that happens within. There is really no need to address what is happening outside of you because all keys and resolutions lie within. When you change your internal reality, your outer reality will shift. What this means is that any situation, any relationship or encounter which is bothering and triggering you needs to be dealt with inside of you. Anything you judge in the world and any cause (environmental, social, political...) you feel drawn to also finds its resolution within you. We do not change the outer reality by working on it but by going within.

If we judge or are bothered, there is something within us to work with. This doesn't mean that it is not out there in the other person we project upon or in the environment we live in - it most certainly is as well by the collective nature of soul. However, it is only in our experience because it is within us to start with.

You may also find this interesting: whatever you do not encounter in your life is also linked to your inner programming as well as your oversoul vibrational path. This doesn't mean it doesn't exist. A simple example would be events which happen far away from you on this very planet or even in your city, but that you do not encounter as part of your life: it is just not part of your experience because you are not programmed for it or it's not part of your spiritual path in this incarnation. So, oneness doesn't mean one has to care for and deal with everything and go out to seek it. Your life brings you all you need to deal with.

Conscious parenting is about mending the garden of your inner work as an adult and that of your child and nurturing the ideal garden daily. This is a complete turnaround of how we conventionally see life: instead of focusing on the outer issues and spending energy in fixing them, changing other people's (including your child's) behaviours and complaining when things don't change or are not the way you want, we are inviting you to use your outer experiences as observation points for you to examine what may be going on inside of you to experience such a reality.

We are also inviting you to put your focused attention on the oversoul and keep planting the ideal garden in yourself by visualising and feeling it from a place of unconditional love and not limitedness. Conscious parenting is about bringing the garden from spirit to matter by consciously choosing where you put your attention (the oversoul), how you take responsibility for your own life and the reality you experience, and how you serve your child by helping them consciously choose where they put their attention (the oversoul), and how they in turn take responsibility for their own life and the reality they experience.

The Conscious Parent Role

As a parent you have two roles in one: being a conscious adult and a conscious parent. The beauty and sweet spot of parenting, as it is on your path, is that much of your personal work to be a conscious adult and progress on your oversoul journey is linked to parenting. So, these are not two separate or consecutive roles, they go hand in hand.

For yourself, being a conscious parent involves self-love towards all of who you are; the balanced embodiment of unconditional love, divine wisdom and power; the healing and clearing of your inner programs which are not serving your highest well-being in this incarnation; the devotion to your spiritual path and the development of divine qualities; the aspiration to reclaim oversoul sovereignty.

Towards your child, being a conscious parent involves the strong (unshakable) intention of standing as a threefold pillar of unconditional love, divine wisdom and power. It also involves a dedicated practice for your child as long as you have their responsibility: observing and identifying what their non serving inner programs are and clearing them for them so you may help them develop a healthy balanced personality; helping the child become conscious of the divine child within and remain in contact with it throughout their growth (read about the divine child in the dedicated chapter); being the space for your child to experience joy, bliss, unconditional love and divine trust. This is in essence what a conscious parent is: a guide and catalyst for unconditional love.

The wisdom of parenting lies in your ability to observe your child and not intervene on their path but help them clear their limitations. This requires that you are able and have examined your own judgements about what is right or wrong for your child, and the humility to trust your child's divine blueprint. For example, a child who has come to shatter the outdated social structures may not have in their divine blueprint to go to university: can you live with it? For example, a child who has already mastered the skills of negotiation may not have in their divine blueprint to go on a path of diplomacy, sales or justice, but instead learn a completely new set of skills and yet they may appear to you as the ideal lawyer or salesperson: can you live with it? Most of the challenge is that – as you discover who your child is and what their blueprint is about as you live together and through the topics of life – your own limitations surface. These are questions parents are invited to ask themselves in every divine now moment and not pre-think.

Stewardship of the Garden

Each of us holds within our consciousness a key to the meaning of the Garden of Eden. It is to live life on Earth in the awareness of the Kingdom of God.

This consciousness exists when all of life is seen as sacred. Each of us lives in God's garden which we are to tend with loving care. Care for ourselves and those within it.

Beloved ones, the task of becoming a parent requires of us that we prevent our inner house and garden - our inner world - from falling into disrepair through neglect or treating it in a manner as if it did not matter.

We nurture our inner world so that our god-self presence may radiate from us in every moment.

Parenting ourselves includes maintaining our inner world in a state of pristine purity. Our god-self presence within is already ready to radiate, our responsibility is to polish the mirrors, clean the surfaces, remove all that would reduce our radiance, so we may shine in God's glory.

Parenting as an Act of Leadership

Working with adults, we have observed how often the node of their transformation lies with their inner child and how the connection to the oversoul through their divine child is life changing.

Imagine how different our world would be if the children of today, who will be the leaders of tomorrow, grew up with a solid anchoring in their oversoul and were parented with firm unconditional love and if the connection to the divine child was nurtured and remained strong throughout childhood and into adulthood.

Conventional parenting disregards the soul level. Conventional leadership also excludes the soul level. Consequently, our societies are plateauing in the personality level, disconnected from the harmonising creative Source within them.

Barbara Ann Brennan states in her book, *Light Emerging: The Journey of Personal Healing* "*Disease is the result of a distortion in our consciousness (our intent) that blocks the expression of our essence from coming through all the levels into the physical. Dis-ease is an expression of how we have tried to separate ourselves from our deeper being, our essence.*" [vii]

Imagine what a difference it will make for humanity if we parent our children and ourselves from this understanding (read more about this in the chapter dedicated to parenting the inner child; see page 180).

Parenting at the soul level and with the understanding of the complete body system, in support of the oversoul's evolution, growth and integration, is an act of leadership towards Self and Child. It takes leadership to pause and renew oneself, to step back from the conventional ways of leading and living life to embrace sourceness.

Story of the One Breath

*There is a story that I would tell you,
my beloved one,
and it is the story of the one Breath,
and how the Creator of All who
breathed out the universe
in all its many forms,
continues to breathe life into it
through the one Breath.
You are breathing in this life at
every moment.
In every moment it is dancing through
you, breathing through you.
You may not feel it,
but this does not prevent it
from moving through you.
When you are aware of this
my beloved one,
you will not only feel joy.
You will feel home.
You will feel a belonging to life
that you may not have felt before.
Breathe in the One Breath,
and know that you are created to do this.
No effort. Just One Breath.*
GurujiMa [viii]

A Word on Betterment and Improvement

In recent years, personal development and growth have gained massive popularity. Most people we meet and work with want to become better and improve themselves. They want to be better leaders, better parents, better family members, better people… There seems to be an insatiable thirst for self-improvement and a collective encouragement of such endeavours.

From the personality perspective, there is a twofold dynamic at play:
- On the one hand, there is a genuine desire to change and experience a different life.
- On the other hand, there is also deep fear rooted in these trends which is mostly unconscious. If you have a desire to improve yourself and become a better version of yourself, we encourage you to examine carefully what is at the root of this desire:
- Is it your oversoul calling?
- Is it your personality urging you to action (out of fear)?

When it comes to conscious parenting, we would like to stress three important points for you to reflect upon:

1) Fear only generates fear.
2) The oversoul does not require improvement. It may require clearing, activating, aligning and harmonising, but it is already perfect and divine. There is nothing to improve in or about it.
3) The personality can improve and become better through your commitment to self-love. By this, we mean changing your personality from one which does not serve your oversoul to one that is in service to your highest well-being in this incarnation and your oversoul service to God and Earth.

PART TWO: FOUNDATIONS – GROUNDING AND ANCHORING (ANCHORED-NESS)

Being ideally connected to Earth and Source are so fundamental in your healthy oversoul journey that we have dedicated a whole section to this topic. Considering the widespread lack of anchoring in both adults and children it is necessary to not only understand why this is such an important foundation, but also how to solidly build it.

The children of today are (mostly because of their template set-up which we wrote about in the foundation part of this book) particularly sensitive to the density of Earth vibrational frequencies and thus find it particularly challenging to ground on Earth. As a consequence, they usually are not anchored/grounded, oftentimes because it would be a painful experience for them. As a parent, you will find that working consciously to accompany your child to anchor and ground will lead to amazing benefits in your and their life.

Chapter 1
Grounding and Anchoring for Parents

A flourishing garden is one where plants and trees are ideally rooted and where the grounds are attentively cared for. Trees grow strong and tall as their roots are deeply and solidly anchored. Healthy soil is necessary for healthy roots. For us humans, this is just as valid. There is no spiritual growth without solid foundations, and this involves grounding and anchoring. Anchoring on Earth is a foundational spiritual step. We have mentioned already that at the spiritual level, Earth and Humanity are one. We need a healthy connection to Earth to function ideally. Being grounded is about touching down and being connected to Earth, allowing Earth's nourishment and energy to flow through us. It is honouring our Earthness.

You have certainly heard about very helpful and highly recommended practices such as walking barefoot on grass or sand, spending time in Nature, forest bathing, swimming in natural waters or gardening / having plants at home. These are fabulous and nourishing practices. They contribute to nourishing your connection, appreciation and gratitude for Earth.

In this chapter, we look at practices that will help you ground your entire being in a sustainable way. It is useful to mention that in recent years the practice of Earth anchoring has evolved substantially, and it may no longer be ideal to ground oneself on the planet itself. We invite you not to assume that grounding down means to ground into planet Earth. You will read more about this in the channelled messages on grounding and anchoring from Telonis (below).

We will share practices to anchor your:
- Pillar of Light
- Central channel
- Four lower bodies
- Oversoul
- Earth Star, Soul Star and Source Star

What is meant by being "grounded'?

A message from Telonis, our guide and teacher:

There is confusion about this term. Yet no need to be confused.

There is a very specific meaning to being grounded.

For our purposes, one is grounded if one is fully connected to this Earth. Anyone who is alive in a physical body, indeed any living thing, plant or animal, requires to be 'grounded' into Earth.

For plants, they are grounded through their root system. Trees have giant root systems. No matter the size of the root system, every plant needs a healthy root system to flourish.

For humans to be grounded they need to be fully connected energetically, through their human energy system into the Earth. Anyone alive will have at minimum, a thread of connection to Earth. But a small thread of connection will not allow the being to thrive because through that small thread, insufficient nurturing energy from Earth (our mother) will be received. Those with very narrow threads or channels of connection often experience health, thriving issues, confusion, intermittent feelings of being connected one minute and 'lost' the next.

To be 'grounded' one needs a solid and fully developed 'root system'. All human beings have roots. They appear and seem different to each of us. For some they look just like plant roots. For others they are crystal shards. For some streams of light substance/plasma.

Not every being here requires this Earth grounding. Some are 'grounded' into the Universe, meaning they have already made their full Earth connection (or not) and are now 'grounded' in another way. It is important to be aware of this as your child may be one of these beings, therefore 'grounding' is a different matter for them. For them, the issue of anchoring may be more relevant.

If, however, you feel that your grounding could be improved, then work on your 'rooting' connection to the Earth first. Eventually we all shift to be 'grounded' in a different way, but we are not all 'wired' like this in the beginning. Why? Because we have chosen to experience a different wiring set-up to begin with.

One wishes you find the ideal way for you to ground into Earth, or wherever is ideal for you.

NB: There are exercises in the Sourceness Journal that will help you with grounding.

What is meant by "anchoring"?

A message from Telonis, our guide and teacher:

Again, there exists some confusion about this term.

Anchoring is your connection to the multiverse. You are a multi-dimensional being who exists outside of what you believe to be time and space. Time and space, as understood by most humans, does not exist in the multiverse.

The multiverse is more like the images and concepts expressed in the movie Dr Strange, but even here that view is limited compared to the true reality. However, we deal with present reality so for most of you the focus that will serve you is on connecting your human energy system into the multiverse in a way that is ideal for you.

Beloved souls you are all unique, and I speak with your soul now as we encourage you to realise that to be the highest expression of All That You Are, 'anchored-ness' is essential.

Anchored-ness' is that presentness state of being anchored. You will each anchor in a unique way.

Anchored means to be fully connected into every divine light structure that is ideal for you, in alignment with divine will, in the divine now moment. And yes, that means that your anchoring changes almost in every divine now moment. The lower mind does not need to concern itself with this work as this anchoring may be 'automated.'

Anchoring into the multiverse is something that you may not be able to see, unless your clairvoyant sensing is developed. However, you will feel it, sense and know it. The way we would explain anchoring is like having a space station that is moving through quantum space. The space station has reinforcing throughout to make it sturdy and resilient; the human energy system has the same. However, the human energy system also has a blueprint, a plan for this life, which is overseen, guided by the soul. This blueprint exerts energy on the human, the being. Like webs/threads of energy holding the human space station in an 'orbit' as it progresses along its 'path'.

There is nothing accidental about the path. There is choice on the path, the human being has free-will on this path, but the blueprint contains all these possibilities. The anchoring into the multiverse maintains equilibrium and balance on the path. It is not meant to dictate; it is designed by Source to gently guide.

Gentle guidance is subtle guidance. Navigating the divine light structures of the multiverse is a simple matter when one is anchored.

You will find in the Sourceness Journal, channelled exercises to help you with anchoring.

Wishing you a joyful experience in exploring the multiverse.

Getting Started

We mentioned earlier about the Spiritual Hierarchy: there are two Archangels who are particularly keen on helping you with grounding and anchoring work: Archangel Sandalphon and Archangel Metatron.

Archangel Sandalphon and his twin flame, Archeia Shekinah, work with Earth Star Chakra energies, as they work with Earth energy.

Lord Metatron and Archeia Sophia work with the Soul Star Chakra and higher transpersonal chakras. Lord Metatron, Lord of Light, also works with the Divine Plan, and oversoul and monad plans for everyone.

Sandalphon works with that divinity on Earth. Sandalphon works with the Earth Star chakra in your energetic field, and Metatron works with the Soul Star chakra.

Sophia works with the divine feminine principle of Divine Love/Wisdom of the cosmos, and Shekinah anchors the "womb" of humanity on Earth.

Calling on Archangel Sandalphon

For all grounding practices and connection to Earth, call upon Archangel Sandalphon to supervise, guide and assist you. Sandalphon will also upgrade light structures and clear blockages in your roots and Earth Star. His light is nourishing and deeply regenerating. He protects and preserves your inner soil. Sandalphon is in direct connection to Metatron, or metaphorically speaking, connecting the Earth and the Skies. In the Hierarchy, Sandalphon is the archangel in charge of uplighting Earth-related light structures so that the Divine Plan can manifest in the material earthly plane.

Calling on Archangel Metatron

You can call on Archangel Metatron to guide and assist you in your anchoring practice to Source and to upgrade, update and heal your light structures or place new light structures around you as is ideal for you in alignment with divine will. Metatron's Light is directly stemming from Source and is of the highest purity. In the Hierarchy, Metatron is in first command and in direct service to Source receiving divine instructions as pure light and oversees bringing divine light into the awareness of people.

Anchoring Your Pillar of Light - Ground and Top

The Pillar of Light is one of the primary light technologies we recommend you work with. It is, as its name suggests, a pillar made of pure light cosmic substance which is all around your body system, including your spiritual bodies. As you begin working with the Pillar of Light, visualise it at least 3 metres wide all around your physical body (it is much wider, but if you can hold the visualisation of it as 3 metres wide, that's wonderful).

The purpose of your Pillar of Light is to protect your energetic integrity. You will find in the *Sourceness Journal* a primary exercise to work with the Pillar of Light and seal it so that denser energies to your vibration can leave your body system and not enter, and only the highest purest light may enter. This is the basic protection you can always maintain, and we cannot stress enough how useful it is to do so. The Pillar of Light is not an advanced light technology and there will be in the future other tools to ensure basic protection and integrity. For now, and this will be the case for a few years still, we highly encourage you to practise daily with the Pillar of Light and have it always sealed.

Anchoring and grounding your Pillar of Light is also part of this daily practice. You want to make sure your Pillar of Light is anchored at the bottom where it is ideal for you in alignment with divine will and at the top in Undifferentiated Source or where it is ideal for you in alignment with divine will. In this way, you are ideally held in integrity.

Having your Pillar of Light anchored at the bottom is of tremendous help for many things such as:
- Focus and concentration.
- Groundedness and Presence.
- Awareness and responsiveness.
- Protection/ Health / Power.
- Growth and integration.

Your Pillar of Light is your foundation, and you want it to be strong, solid and healthy. When your Pillar of Light is not anchored into Earth, you can experience:
- Light-headedness, headache and nausea.
- Confusion and fogginess.
- Insufficient energy and exhaustion.
- Moodiness.

Having your Pillar of Light anchored at the top enables you to:
- Receive ideal flow of Light continuously.
- Be connected to your spiritual dimension and strengthen your connection to Source.
- Experience joy, Divine Light, Love, Wisdom and Power.
- Grow spiritually and integrate your learnings.

When your Pillar of Light is not anchored at the top, you can experience:
- Energy loss.
- Stagnation and lack of growth and integration.
- Disconnection for your oversoul and Divine.

You may request the Pillar of Light anchoring several times a day at the beginning of your practice so that you become aware of the difference for you when your Pillar of Light is anchored and when not.

You will find these, and other exercises related to the Pillar of Light in the *Sourceness Journal* and recorded meditations are also available at www.sourceness.one for you to practise.

Pillar of Light Meditation

Time: Less than 2 minutes.
(recorded version available on www.sourceness.one)

Preparing your Pillar of Light is an essential tool to help you to navigate the energies of now.

The Pillar of Light is a divine light structure. We each have one and it is like a translucent shower curtain which exists all around us and is made of cosmic light substance.

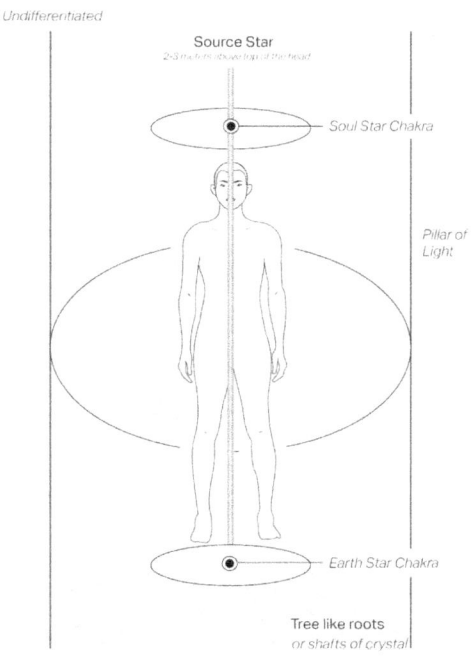

Diagram 13. Pillar of Light

Within the Pillar of Light is the energy that you are, your energy system (this is a construct to help us understand in the beginning what our energy system is).

The Pillar of Light is protective - the divine light structure that it is is made of substance that prevents non-balanced energies from entering our energy system, it lets in only PURE SOURCE light energy, only electrons which are PURE SOURCE charged.

Our Pillar of Light allows any energy that does not serve us to exit from within the Pillar and it prevents it from coming back inside our energy system

The Pillar of Light is supportive - inside our Pillar of Light our divine spark radiates support, love, comfort, compassion, etc.

This quick meditation will activate your Pillar of Light and it will work, even if you 'zone out' while listening, and even if you don't understand it. Nothing is being done to you in this mediation. All in this book operates under the Law of Free Will - meaning if it is not for you, it will not apply to you. And under the intention that 'what is offered is for your highest well-being in alignment with divine will.' Therefore, if it is not for your highest well-being, and/or not in alignment with divine will, it won't apply to you.

Let us begin.

Find a comfortable spot and sit or lie down.

Take a deep breath in. Breathe in the purest light from within you and from without.

Welcome. Accept. Allow. Absorb, all that is the purest light.

Now with your intention, say to yourself aloud or silently the following affirmations:

"I am sealing, sealing, sealing my Pillar of Light as is ideal for me.'

"I am always surrounded by a Pillar of Light, pure and true, which protects me completely, infinitely and forever."

That's it. Your Pillar of Light is now activated.

Clearing the Physical, Emotional Desire and Astral, Mental and Etheric Bodies

Time: less than 5 minutes. For parents. Recording available: www.sourceness.one.

This clearing exercise is for your physical, etheric, emotional, lower and higher mental bodies.

Find a comfortable spot and sit or lie down.

Take a deep breath in. Breathe in the purest light from within you and from without.

Welcome. Accept. Allow. Absorb, all that is the purest light.

Breathe out releasing any energy that no longer serves you, releasing down into the Earth.

Repeat this conscious breath three times.

Say the soul mantra three times.

And state the following:

"I am (as the oversoul") calls on my team in Spirit, oversoul, monad, body elemental and the Lord of Arcturus and the Arcturians, guided and overseen by my monad, for the complete cleansing and purification of my physical, emotional, lower and higher mental and etheric bodies."

Physical Body

To clear your physical body:

- For my physical body, I am requests that all diseases be completely removed and returned to Source as is divine ideal including all negative bacteria, viruses, fungus, cancer, tumours and genetic weaknesses."
- I am requests full permanent imprinting of the divine monadic-blueprint body and mayavarupa body to reign forever in divine ideal."
- I am now wills this innovation for my present emotional/astral body."
- I am asks that all negative emotions, lower-self desire, astral entities and negative psychic energies of all forms and all types that are not the Christ/Buddha archetype be removed."
- I am asks Source for this."

When your physical and astral bodies are clear, then move to the mental bodies.

- I am now wills this invocation for my lower and higher mental body."
- I am requests a complete clearing of my lower and higher mental body."
- I am asks that all dis-empowering ego and imbalanced thought forms be removed and returned to Source and banished from my consciousness, lower and higher mental bodies forever."
- I am requests that all remaining thought forms left in my conscious, subconscious and superconscious minds be only of divine ideal."
- I am requests a complete clearing and repair of my etheric body."
- I am asks that all etheric mucus in my etheric body be immediately removed and returned to Source and that my etheric body be restored to divine ideal and divine blueprint."
- I am is grateful to and thanks my team in Spirit, soul, monad, body elemental and the Lord Metatron and Lord of Arcturus and the Arcturians for their assistance, healing and support in this matter."

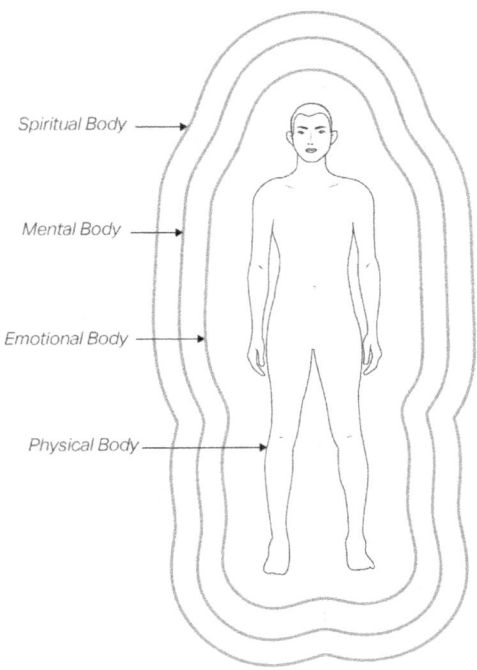

Diagram 14. The Four Bodies

Anchoring Your Central Channel

The central channel, also called Antahkarana Bridge, is the cord of light which connects your oversoul to Earth through your physical body system. As we have mentioned earlier, for most adults today, this cord needs to be consciously activated while most children today already come into incarnation with their central channel partially activated. There are exercises in the *Sourceness Journal* to build and work with your central channel. It is also important that this channel is ideally anchored.

After you have anchored your Pillar of Light and in a similar fashion, you can request the anchoring of your central channel both at the bottom and at the top. It is important that your central channel be anchored down into Earth, and you can request Archangel Sandalphon to do this as is in divine ideal for you.

You will find exercises in the *Sourceness Journal* that will help you, as well as recorded meditations to practice.

Anchoring Your Body System

Depending on which body system you work with, you can request to anchor your four-body system or your five-body system. Please do so after you have sealed and anchored your Pillar of Light and anchored your central channel.

In addition, it is also essential – for most people* - to ground the physical body in Earth and you can do so through:
- The energetic roots below your feet - consciously sending them down into the hollow heart of Earth and receiving back blue green telluric energy (which often translates with a sensation of aliveness in your lower legs).
- Walking barefoot and consciously making the connection to Earth as your feet touch the ground.
- Spending time in nature - which has multiple other benefits such as harmonising your nervous system and regulating your heartbeat as well as detoxifying your aura.
- Stating your intention: "My physical body is ideally anchored in Earth in every divine now moment".

*Some people do not require this. If you are unsure get in touch through www.sourceness.one and we can advise and guide you.

Anchoring Your Earth Star

The Earth Star is the chakra which connects you to Earth and for most people it is just below your feet. Ideal anchoring includes that of your Earth Star. You can request help from Archangel Sandalphon to ideally light up and anchor your Earth Star. You will find how to do this practice in the *Sourceness Journal*.

After you have anchored your Earth Star it is also recommended to check and make sure that your Earth Star and Crown chakras are ideally aligned and connected. This mirrors the alignment of Sandalphon and Metatron.

Observing When Your Anchoring/Grounding Needs Update

From time to time our anchoring and grounding changes. Observing when your anchoring/grounding is not ideal is of great help and oftentimes a first go-to-point when you begin feeling off-balance. The following are signs that anchoring/grounding down is off:
- You feel lightheaded and wobbly
- You cannot feel energy in your feet and lower legs
- you feel as if you were floating and unable to tend your daily tasks
- it seems difficult to concentrate
- you feel overwhelmed

    The following are signs that anchoring/grounding up is off:
- you feel lightheaded and wobbly
- you have a (slight) headache

- you feel unable to concentrate and process information
- you feel foggy or unclear
- you feel out of balance
- you feel confused

These may also be symptoms of other issues as well, but it is wise to first check your anchoring, beginning with the Pillar of Light and central channel, and then moving on to your lower body system and Earth Star. If you find it difficult to know whether you are ideally anchored or not, we suggest you begin by doing the exercises as if you were requesting ideal anchoring/grounding and observe how your internal state changes as you do so. We guarantee that with practice you will soon learn to realise by yourself when your anchoring is off.

Grounding Your Oversoul on Planet Earth

Grounding the oversoul is a very helpful practice that helps your spiritual bodies to descend in your physical reality and thus directly connect and work with Earth, creating a harmonious energy flow between your oversoul and planet Earth in your physical body structure.

You will find the description of the practice in the *Sourceness Journal* and you can do this practice daily.

Here is what you will experience after grounding regularly your oversoul on Earth:
- Greater clarity about who you are and what you have come to do on Earth in this incarnation.
- A stronger connection to planet Earth and nature.
- The experience of love pouring through you into Earth and being nourished by Earth
- Greater harmony in your life.

Chapter 2
Grounding and Anchoring for Children

We cannot stress enough how important it is to ground and anchor down and up not only yourself, but also your children.

This chapter offers a process to initiate and gradually anchor your child in a way that makes it easy for them. It includes specific tools to assist children who find the vibration of Earth painful and have therefore issues "touching down" on Earth.

Learning to observe if your child's Pillar of Light and central channel are ideally anchored down and up is of wonderful help to support your child's well-being. With practice, you will notice rather quickly when the anchoring is off. Until then, we suggest you assume that your child needs anchoring on a daily basis (you cannot over-anchor your child) and the more you consciously request anchoring, the stronger it becomes.

Once you have established anchoring down and up and have a practice of checking your anchoring, you will not feel harmonious if your anchors are off. Likewise for your child: you will observe an increase in their well-being once this anchoring is in place. It's like brushing teeth: if you have a hygiene habit of brushing your teeth daily (as we are sure you do), skipping it even a day feels off. So first you and then your child.

A Word on Anchoring / Grounding and ADHD

In recent years, the medical profession has identified a mental disorder called Attention Deficit Hyperactivity Disorder.

ADHD is a condition that affects people's behaviour. People with ADHD can seem restless, may have trouble concentrating and may act on impulse.

According to the NHS: https://www.nhs.uk/conditions/attention-deficit-hyperactivity-disorder-adhd/. Symptoms of ADHD tend to be noticed at an early age and may become more noticeable when a child's circumstances change, such as when they start school. Most cases are diagnosed when children are under 12 years old, but sometimes it's diagnosed later in childhood. Sometimes ADHD was not recognised when someone was a child, and they are diagnosed later as an adult. The symptoms of ADHD may improve with age, but many adults who were diagnosed with the condition at a young age continue to experience issues. People with ADHD may also have additional problems, such as sleep and anxiety disorders.

We are strongly guided to mention here that with ADHD there is nearly always some kind of anchoring issue. We encourage parents who know/suspect their children to have ADHD or whose child has been labelled as such by the medical profession, to give priority to the grounding and anchoring work described in this material. Dedicated healing and energetic restructuring work will clear any blockage and restore the appropriate energy flows for the child. The patterns of disconnection and the general healing process are described in this book. This energetic restructuring work may also be applicable to a parent(s). We also recommend checking your child's core wound and core crime – exercises for identifying and healing these are in the *Sourceness Journal.*

Patterns of Earth Disconnection with Children

The following list describes various patterns of Earth disconnection. However, it is important to mention that you first need to clarify if it is ideal for your child to be grounded and anchored on Earth because it may not be.

If it is ideal and you face grounding/anchoring challenges for your child, then please explore the following list to identify which pattern they may be on.

There are several patterns which block children from anchoring on Earth:

1) The child doesn't want to be here on Earth because of cellular memories of previous painful experiences (likely past lives which were traumatic). The conclusion in the personality is: "Earth is painful, I don't want to be here"

2) The child finds it difficult to be on Earth because of the discrepancy between the high vibration of his template and the density/'slowness' of Earth. The conclusion in the personality is: "Earth is too dense, too slow and boring. It has nothing to do with me, it has nothing for me".

3) The child is disconnected from Earth because of a deeply ingrained pattern of withdrawal due to dis connection from Divine Love (oftentimes experienced as lack of Self-Love). The conclusion in the personality is: "Earth doesn't love me. I am not welcome. I'd rather not be here".

4) The child finds it difficult to be on Earth because of Earth's imperfections compared to the perfection of God. Earth is just not good enough. The conclusion in the personality is: "I am not good enough being here. Earth is mediocre".

5) The child disconnects from Earth because of cellular memories of previous Trust issues/betrayal which makes relationships dangerous. The conclusion in the personality is: "Earth is dangerous. It's not safe to be here".

6) The child is disconnected and unable to anchor into Earth because of a severe wound of separation with the Divine. The conclusion in the personality is: "I am alone, Earth is a stranger".

7) The child carries the painful memory of past crimes and painful deeds and is unable to forgive one self: "I am bad, I cannot be here on earth".

As you can see, there are judgements involved and memories of past painful experiences which have not been healed. If your child is currently incarnated it is a clear sign that the oversoul is ready to face these challenges. Your empowering attitude and deep trust in the resolution will help the soul and personality of your child alongside your patience to tackle the challenges with unconditional love and respect for the divine timing of their resolution.

If your child is operating on such a pattern, no matter how much you anchor them on Earth, they will disconnect again and again until the pattern is resolved. In some cases, anchoring on Earth can be so scary to the four lower bodies of the child that it is not ideal to do so until the deeper issue is resolved. This requires your careful attention.

The first and most essential step is in recognizing which is the pattern. You can observe their behaviour and listen to the cues they may give.

We recommend that you do not rush this process. It may take many months of work to fully reach anchoring for your child and a healer's support is likely needed. On your side this is a process of investigation and continued infusion of your child's body system with unconditional love.

Helping Your Child Anchor on Earth

Whether or not and while the above process is ongoing, there are a number of things you can do as a parent, to help the anchoring process of your child down into Earth provided it is ideal for them. The following practices will support the ideal grounding and anchoring of your child.

Anchoring the Four Lower Body System in the Upper Heart

This is the first step to take in the process of anchoring your child's body system on Earth. Most children born on Earth at this time already have an activated higher heart, while their parents need to consciously activate their higher heart. The higher heart chakra is the gateway to the heart of God and most children currently on Earth will feel comfortable with that very high frequency energy. As we have mentioned earlier, it is only in rare cases that a child in this time has a disconnection to Source above.

You will find this practice in the *Sourceness Journal*. This is a gentle practice for your child which will bring relief to their entire body system and reinforce trust in their incarnation. A regular anchoring in the higher heart will also ensure the nourishment of the thymus gland and its health.

Balancing the Central Channel (Antahkarana Bridge) of Your Child

The second step is to adjust the central channel of your child. While adults need to actively build their central channel, marking their conscious intention to build the connection to the

Divine in them, most children in this time already come with a partially activated Antahkarana Bridge. Although you have already anchored it (both up and down), it may not be ideally sized, shaped and located. It is likely that in some parts at least, it needs widening and reinforcing. When the central channel is ideally balanced, the divine energy can flow naturally and unconstrained, sustaining the child as it is meant to do.

You will find in the *Sourceness Journal* the process to balance your child's central channel and ensure it is functioning ideally for them. As their parent and while they are under your responsibility, it is up to you to request this work which is part of the foundational energetic wiring of your child.

Placing Your Child in an Adjustment Chamber for Grounding

To address the gap in vibrational frequencies between your child and Earth, the adjustment chamber process can help to remove the pain involved. As mentioned, some children are running on a template which makes it very challenging for them to anchor on the current density of vibration on planet Earth. While planet Earth is increasing her vibration drastically, these children are operating at a higher frequency, making the physical anchoring difficult. Even if your child is not meant to be anchored down on Earth, placing them in an adjustment chamber may be helpful to balance the energies.

This process aims at creating adjustment so that the experience of being on Earth for these children is not so painful. It is like a calibration chamber or an energetic transformer: it will tune down their vibration to match Earth frequency.

We highly recommend you request this chamber for your child, especially if they show a pattern of:

- High sensitivity
- Restlessness
- Crankiness
- Daydreaming, inattention and being absent

This process can be done at any time even before you have started any other anchoring work. You will find in the *Sourceness Journal* the instructions to put the Earth adjustment chamber in place and activate an automatic filtering process to ensure that it is ideal for your child in every divine now moment. In addition, it is recommended to place a cleansing vortex of energy below the chamber to continually remove dense energy that may come into your child from Earth through the anchoring. You will also find this process in the *Sourceness Journal*.

This chamber needs regular upgrading to continue functioning ideally for your child along his/her evolutionary path.

Harmonising Your Child's Earth Star Chakra

As you read earlier, the Earth Star is the chakra which connects you to Earth and for most people is approximately 1.5 metres below the feet into the ground. To help your child in their process of accepting and adjusting to incarnation on planet Earth, you can harmonise and balance their Earth Star chakra. You will find this process in the *Sourceness Journal.*

PART THREE: THE THREE PILLARS OF PARENTING (STRUCTUREDNESS)

The foundations we use in this book to hold the garden are the Three Pillars of Love, Wisdom and Power. These three pillars are integrated within each one of us as a divine flame which burns in our heart. As such, it is not a pillar we need to build or acquire but rather aspects of ourselves (our divine selves) to reconnect, to revive, and nurture.

Throughout our human history we have believed that Love, Wisdom and Power are aspirations to seek and possess. We have also adhered to illusions such as:

- "Love is an enchantment" - as in expression falling in love
- "Power is a conquest" - as we experience in the history of nations for millennia or in the business world
- "Wisdom is knowledge" - as portrayed in allegories of old bearded men with books.

These are all examples of thought forms that alter our direct perception of love, power and wisdom. It is not to say, for example, that love cannot be an enchantment. However, if we confine our experience of love to the consensus reality of mass consciousness, we are greatly limiting ourselves.

In this chapter we will look at each pillar from the personality level (soul extension) and from the oversoul level.

From the Personality Level:

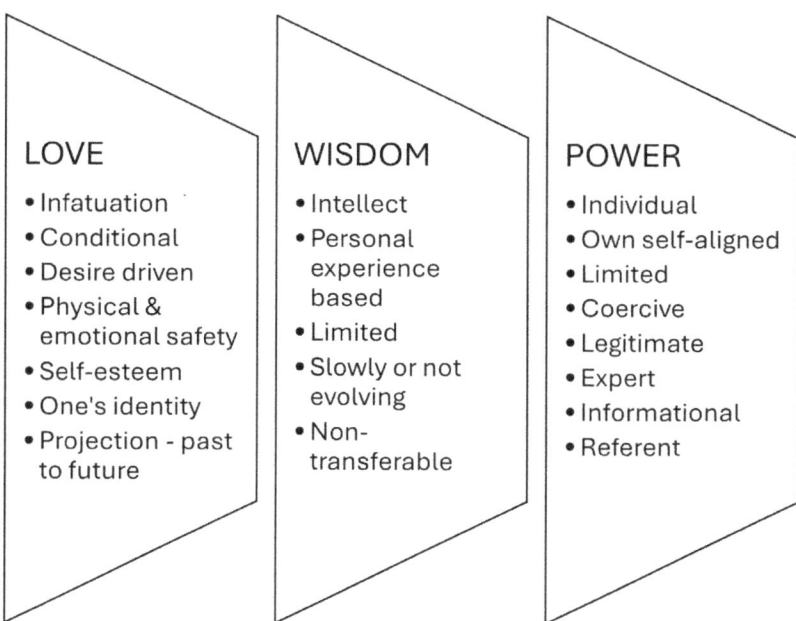

- Love = self-love vs. lack of self-love generating an emptiness the personality strives to fill.
- Wisdom = knowledge vs. ignorance.
- Power = force vs. impotence.

As you can see, at the personality level each pillar has a higher and lower expression, or more accurately two polarities. Every quality experienced at the personality level has a polarity by the very nature of the personality which cannot perceive the wholeness of transcended duality.

From the Oversoul Level:

- Love = Divine Unconditional Love.
- Wisdom = Divine/Universal Wisdom.
- Power = Divine Will & Power.

From an Integrated Perspective:

All three pillars when integrated at the oversoul level operate as one force. A fully integrated garden is Love, Wisdom and Power all three operating in service to your sourceness.

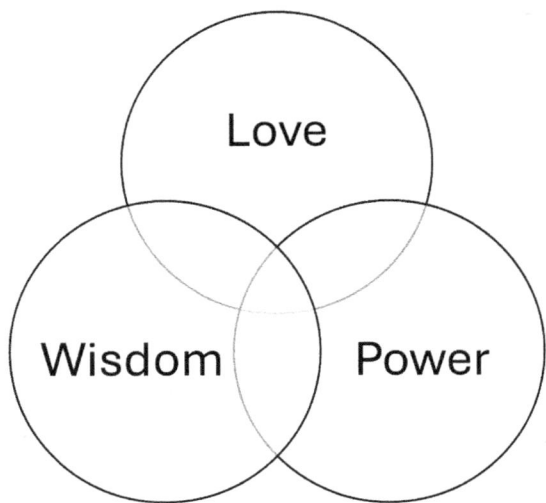

We will investigate each pillar at the level of personality and soul.

Chapter 1
Pillar 1: LOVE / Self Love and Unconditional Love

What we understand, focus on and experience of love is different at the personality level and at the soul level. Let's look at it through both lenses and clarify what we mean when we talk about Love as the first pillar of parenting in this book.

Love at the Personality Level

At the personality level, love is about self-love and the aspiration is to complete 100% Self Love. What we mean by this is that every aspect of your personality is operating out of love for Self. A healthy personality loves itself and does not leave any space for anything which is not love. This involves transmuting / clearing / removing the blockages and programs you hold in your four lower bodies to experience the highest loving sense of self available to you.

There are two challenges involved with Love at the personality level which we bring to your attention:

1) All of us have experienced pain and suffering and carry to some extent unprocessed hurts from other lives which leave our personality bucket filled with limiting conclusions and programs. There are many layers to these unprocessed hurts and full healing requires that you deal with them all the way down to the universal core wound you have identified with and carry in your body system.
2) Our society is obsessed with love and more precisely the lack of it. This generates continuous messaging of hurt and fear which you are likely exposed through media, social media, music and film industries, entertainment…

Developing Love at the Personality Level

It is important to fully understand, realise, accept and integrate that there is nothing inherently wrong or faulty about you in any way, and at the personality level any lack of love you experience (in both giving and receiving love) is due to your programming from conclusions you have drawn in your multiple incarnations and have not updated. Lack of self-love is constructed by yourself. Love at the personality level is about:
- Physical safety, appreciation, closeness and intimacy
- Emotional safety, harmony, free expression and connection
- Self-esteem and positive self-image

Developing Love at the Personality Level

- Self-esteem and positive self-image
- Appreciation of one's identity
- Healing the personality bucket

The highest expression of love at the personality level is 100% Self Love in all the dimensions of you and life. It is what enables us to say, know, feel, sense that:

- "We are enough and have enough"
- "We are valuable and worthy"
- "We are safe"
- "We are capable"
- "We are loved".

This means that we stop feeding the personality's programs which make us seek completion, appreciation, harmony, self-esteem, recognition, fulfilment and love… outside of us in some quest, other person, or group, or activity. Seeking in any way compensation for a lack of self-love outside of you will only leave you depleted and reinforce a sense of emptiness.

A healthy personality is not an empty well of love and it is part of the foundational work of your garden to ensure that your physical, emotional and lower mental bodies are not starving for love but are ideally nourished and nurtured. Every time you observe a lack of self-love in you and cut through its illusion, you restore love within yourself.

There are exercises in the *Sourceness Journal* designed to help you build and develop 100% self-love.

Healing Love at the Personality Level

By design, the personality or individual self sees themself as separated from others. Unity is lived at the soul level and not by the personality. As we have also mentioned, the challenge of love at the personality level is to transmute any lack or distortion of it back to 100% self-love which is the natural state of a healthy personality.

However, this is often not the starting point for most of you. At the personality level, we ask questions or hold beliefs such as:

- Is it safe to love?
- What if I get hurt?
- I experienced pain before; will it happen again?
- I love you and do you love me back?
- Am I lovable to you?
- Will I ever be enough?

Healing Love at the Personality Level

- If you behave a certain way, then I will love you / If I behave a certain way, then you will love me.
  How are my behaviours?
- I have a right to not love him/her when they... What are my narratives?
- If I belong to this group, I am loved. Am I belonging?
- Am I enough to belong, to be loved?
- ...

All these questions are personality narratives based on fear and highlight a lack of love in one or more of the four lower bodies. From an energetic perspective, they correspond to the first three lower chakras: the base/root chakra, the polarity/sacral chakra and the solar plexus chakra.

Three Lower Chakras

The Root Chakra

The root chakra is the seat of the physical body. It oversees safety and groundedness.

In this chakra, we deal with issues of safety, acceptance of being here on Earth, grounding. It is a very primal chakra, and it deals with the primal fear of separation from the divine, unity, oneness, the mother. This chakra is also tied to raw, non-emotional sexual energy, the animal sexual impulse in the human being. When you work and process the conclusions your personality has made in this chakra, you establish the foundations of safety within you and tame the animal self.

The Sacral Chakra

The sacral chakra is the chakra of emotions and polarity. It oversees our creativity and balance; it deals with emotional sexual energies. This chakra has a front and a back: the front side deals with our emotions and the back side is the seat of our subconscious mind. The sacral chakra is strongly connected with the astral plane, with a very strong "illusion making" power. For example, when you face a situation and make a distorted story of it in your mind, convinced that you have seen the reality and thus get carried into an inner drama with intense emotions, you are experiencing the illusion making power of the sacral chakra. When you work and process the conclusions your personality has drawn in this chakra, you build discernment, reduce the need and care for emotional drama, as well as establish harmony and balance in your life. A healthy sacral chakra is stable and harmonious, ideally balancing the polarities.

Solar Plexus

The solar plexus chakra is the seat of the personality's will. This refers to your free will as a human being to choose and take decisions with or without alignment with divine will. This chakra also has a front and a back. The front corresponds to the emotional side of free will, while the back is the mental side. A healthy solar plexus enables one to experience self-esteem and to make decisions which are tempered and in service to one's highest well-being. When you work and process the conclusions your personality has made in this chakra, the personality gets more attuned to love rather than fear, and this enables the opening and activation of the heart chakra.

The healing journey of self-love involves working with these three chakras and clearing the non-serving programs stored in your four lower bodies for this incarnation. When you have cleared and released blockages in the root, sacral and solar plexus chakras, then they can function ideally and be conduits of love. You then experience safety, openness to be in relationship with others, a healthy self-esteem and eagerness to explore life, express yourself. This enables the activation and opening of the heart chakra. At the personality level, there are always circumstances when we deny or withdraw love and so it is not unconditional: personality love is conditional even when you have healed all limiting programs and blockages. However, when the terrain of the personality is sufficiently healthy, meaning you have worked and processed the issues and limitations of your first three chakras, the oversoul can begin to come in, even if you are still partially personality led.

The personality itself can crave for divine love, infatuating itself with illusions, without ever being able to surrender and instead can become obsessed, agitated, even mad for a projection, an image, an idolisation of love it cannot reach. It is part of your healing work to recognize the personality's attachment to ideas and illusions of love. For many of us, we have had an innate knowing of divine love, but we have suppressed, negated and separated ourselves from it to survive, fit in and function in society throughout ages. It is in service to yourself, your children and humanity at large to heal these issues and radiate unconditional love.

Love at The Soul Level

At the soul level, we are Love divine, and have the intrinsic knowing, sensing, feeling of it, unconditional, bountiful, ubiquitous. Divine Love is not dependent on anything: inner or outer conditions, events, circumstances, agreements, loyalties, vows, statements, behaviours, attitudes, mindsets, values… It is also not reserved to a group or kin, it is radiating to all.
Divine Love is not personal: "I love you" is irrelevant because at the soul level, the interconnectedness of all that is - things and beings - is predominant over the individual. I love or I am Love. Love simply is. It is a state of beingness. As a reminder, at the soul level, you are collective

and not a single soul extension.

We all have an inner knowing of Divine Love which we are. However, if we are operating at the personality level, we do not realise this: the constructed limitations of our multi-layered identity block the view, like an enchantment which prevents us from seeing what is right in front of us, what we actually are and have always been.

When we talk about love in this book, what we mean is love at the soul level: Divine Love, unconditional, unrestricted, unconstrained, infinite and eternal. This is the love you are at the soul level and the one which we are inviting you to anchor in your parenting.

Accessing and Radiating Unconditional Love

As mentioned, to prepare the oversoul to reclaim its sovereignty, your work is to transmute and process in the four lower chakras the conclusions your personality has made which are no longer serving you in this incarnation.

For most adults, this process also involves the conscious activation of your upper heart chakra: our societies have so widely disregarded this chakra that although it is present in everyone at birth, it has gone dormant in most adults. The children of today, however, come to life with an active upper heart and it is the role of the parents to keep this chakra open and healthy. So, we will distinguish in this book between two heart chakras, and we will call them out of simplicity as the lower heart and the upper heart.

The lower heart chakra is the seat of love at the personality level. When you work and process the non-serving conclusions of your personality in the first three chakras we introduced (root, sacral, solar plexus), the lower heart opens and activates. In this chakra, you develop the base for compassion with yourself and others. The lower heart chakra is in the central chest area and is associated with the heart which serves the pumping and distribution function of blood in the body. This chakra doesn't have much to do with unconditional love apart from serving as a bridge into the upper heart.

The higher heart chakra is the seat of unconditional love, it is your oversoul's heart chakra. The higher heart is the bridge to divine love: to see / feel / sense / know through the heart/mind of God, you need to work with this chakra. To experience unconditional love, you need to grow and mature this chakra. Most people still believe that the lower heart chakra is the gateway to divine love, and this is not the case. The higher heart chakra is located between your collarbones and is associated with the thymus gland.

Radiating unconditional love involves the activation, opening and nourishment of your higher heart chakra. You will find in the *Sourceness Journal* exercises to do so. We cannot stress enough how important it is that you work with your upper heart and stop associating only the lower heart with love.

Why Unconditional Love?

Unconditional love radiates from us when we fully allow it. It is allowing this radiance to flow to someone no matter what they do and having no expectation of repayment but knowing that energy flows in all ways... and so will flow back to us.

This simple radiance of loving someone unconditionally without any concern of how it may benefit may activate the same parts of the brain that lights up when you show romantic and maternal love according to 2009 research. In other words, unconditional love can benefit you even though you're not expecting anything in return when giving love to others.

Radiating unconditional love can be good for you. Research from 2021* has found that both giving and receiving love can play a crucial role in your psychological well-being, especially later in life.

Research from 2010* suggests receiving unconditional love can also have an impact on your emotional well-being. Findings indicate that children who receive high levels of nurture and love from their parents at a young age tend to have less distress in adulthood as well as fewer mental health symptoms.

Unconditional love can also provide a sense of security. "You are free to be yourself and express your needs without fear of judgement," explains New York Psychologist, David Tzall. You know someone is on your side and looking out for your best interests. You're also secure that they won't leave during rough times. "Unconditional love promotes trust, and trust and security go hand in hand."

Chapter 2
Pillar 2: WISDOM/Knowledge, Discernment and Divine Wisdom

Through the embodiment of unconditional love, we build wisdom.

The golden key to distinguish between personality level wisdom and Divine Wisdom is spiritual discernment which we build through observation in the moment through the lens of unconditional love. We build discernment when for example: we identify how conditional our love is; we identify that our awareness has been captured by automatic programming; we notice that our emotions are taking over our oversoul's sovereignty, hampering our ability to respond.

In other words, discernment is not a content nor a checklist, but rather an active (detached) observation of ourselves which leads us to consciously choose our response to a situation - inner or outer - from a place of alignment within ourselves. This alignment tunes us to our divine relative truth in every divine now moment. When we stand in our wisdom, our oversoul gains gravitas and we become a beacon of stability for our children to rely on (and others around us as well): we are not doing anything, we are just being in our wisdom.

Our children do not learn our wisdom for they have to grow their own in their own relative divine truth. However, whenever wisdom is anchored in sourceness, it is radiating truth-ness and our children recognize it inherently.

To access divine wisdom, we need to become aware of the limitations we have put on ourselves, for what we call wisdom at the personality level is not enabling us to access our divine relative truth.

Wisdom at the Personality Level

Wisdom at the personality level is what we conventionally understand by wisdom: knowledge.

It is the result of analysing, comparing, organising, structuring, learning from data, past events, experimenting, projecting into the future, studying cause and effect... Such knowledge has been widely valued by human societies throughout ages and for this reason, there are deeply anchored thoughtforms which relate to it.

The following is a list of the most prominent thought forms about knowledge:
- The more knowledge, the more intelligent
- The more knowledge, the more successful
- Knowledge is power
- Knowledge is success
- If you know you belong
- Knowledge is reserved to a few
- If you don't know, you'd better be silent

- If you don't know, you're missing out
- The unknowing are not worthy

Such thought forms are part of the collective conclusions of humanity and need addressing as they do not serve our collective evolution. Wisdom at the personality level is also the knowledge you have personally gained through your own experiences, learnings, your upbringing and the beliefs which have formed your identity. For example, "if you drink a glass of warm milk, you will sleep better". Personality level wisdom can only be limited to knowledge and the intelligence of the lower mind which works through cause and effect and categorisation / prioritisation / analysis... It cannot, by design, access divine wisdom.

Wisdom at the Soul Level

Divine Wisdom

Divine Wisdom or Wisdom at the soul level (oversoul, monad) is not building up on any past knowledge and is not related to the conclusions of your personality. It also does not operate like the lower mind in cause and effect / analysis thinking.

Soul level wisdom is directly connected to Source, fuelled with unconditional love and is all encompassing, all knowing, eternal and ubiquitous. Source is omniscient.

Soul level wisdom is experienced in the present now moment when you are attuned to your oversoul. It doesn't give you knowledge but is nourishing your inner knowingness (being in a state of knowing). All the wisdom you need to access in every divine now moment is readily available to your soul. This is so for everyone.

Every time we learn one of the lessons our oversoul has set itself to learn on its evolutionary path, we enrich ourselves with greater wisdom and is a stepping stone towards greater challenges and experiences. The wisdom we carry in our oversoul and which we consciously become aware of helps the personality to be surrendered to the oversoul. Every soul level wisdom when we access it, becomes a landmark and a compass in our life.

Spiritual Discernment

The muscle to develop to access Divine Wisdom is spiritual discernment, an in the moment truth detector. We grow from wherever we are. Pretending to be somewhere we are not, does not serve us because when we try to move forward, we are likely to be confused, heading in directions that are in authentic.

The more conscious you are in every moment, the more discernment you will be able to cultivate, aware of what is happening in your life and consciously being able to choose how you respond. We are not free to respond when we are running on automatic mode, letting existing programs guide us and inner or outer rules dictate our behaviour. We are not aware of what is really happening when we follow the train of our thoughts, our collective conditioning and suffer the surge of our emotions; we are not in spiritual discernment when we operate from the personality level.

To practise spiritual discernment effectively, you must be honest with yourself.
- What do you really want?
- How deep are you willing to go?
- What are your true motivations?

There is no use pretending to be one thing and behaving in the opposite way. Eventually, you'll be called out by yourself, others, or Life itself.

Spiritual discernment works when you are first crystal clear about your own internal personality level drives and desires and are honest with yourself. This enables you to access distortion-free guidance of your oversoul. As you welcome and follow it, you build wisdom.

Developing Spiritual Discernment Levels to Navigate Where you are

Developing spiritual discernment is a process and practice. For many, doubt (e.g., am I getting this right?) and unconscious programming (which has other goals than listening to the oversoul) gets in the way. The following aims at giving you an idea of the level of development you can gradually build.

First level of discernment: is to observe through the lens of which level you are operating: personality level or soul level and consciously step in the soul level.

Personality level discernment is to observe who is in charge of your four-body system. If you are identified with your thoughts or emotions or physical sensations, then you are discerning from your personality - you are identifying with the situation or experience.

Oversoul/monad level discernment. If you are observing in a detached manner, meaning you are observing what is happening or what is being experienced as if watching from a distance, and you dispassionately observe, for example, that 'there is manipulation taking place', then you are oversoul/monad level discerning.

Second level of discernment is to observe from the soul level, what is going on underneath what you observe: Is it aligned with divine will? Is it a judgement? Is it fear? Is it a program? Is it external energy in you? Is it malevolent? ... This is like diagnostic making from the soul level.

Third level of discernment is when you observe what is going on from a dispassionate place of detachment and you can sense / see / hear / feel / know the illusion underlying what you observe. You see through glamour, illusion and maya. [ix]

The fourth level of discernment is when you can observe what is going on / being experienced with dispassionate detachment, can receive guidance about 'what the divine wills in this instance' and receive guidance about what process you are guided to work with to address the situation.

At the highest level, spiritual discernment operates from Christ Consciousness.

It is not important at which level you are, but that you honestly recognize it and work towards the next stage, dispassionately but with great commitment.

Chapter 3
Pillar 3: POWER / Free Will and Divine Will and Power

The third pillar of parenting is Power, and it involves personal power and free will at the personality level and divine will and Power at the soul level.

Power is an essential pillar of creation: without power, there would be no experiencing of our intentions, dreams and aspirations. It is the drive of power that manifests intentions into matter.

Power is a fiery energy, and it can light up just as it can burn down. It can build up just like it can destroy. When it comes to Power, spiritual discernment is also necessary: what can be seen from one perspective as tragic may be seen from another as balancing, healing, transformative.

A Word About Intentions

A message from Telonis:

Greetings dear ones.

A foundation for conscious action is intention.

Why is intention important?

In the beginning of your journey, you will be operating from personal will and so intention flows from what you personally wish to experience in this life.

You may intend to follow your desires, preferences, without realising that these may not be aligned with your soul guided blueprint. And this is fine. All human beings on Earth have free will.

As you shift to a more soul centred approach and begin to develop a soul-to-soul relationship, the 'voice of the soul' seeks to influence these intentions. The soul is aligned with divine will as is your blueprint.

Which comes first, your willingness to align to your soul blueprint or your intention to follow its guidance? Well, that is up to you. However, setting clear intentions can bring alignment with your blueprint and once one is in alignment, guidance becomes clearer.

We encourage you, from time to time, to check in with yourself about your intentions.

For now, how do these intentions resonate?

Personality level intentions:

I intend opening my subconscious mind to guidance as to how I may parent in a soul-to-soul relationship.

This intention speaks to the posture of your subconscious mind.

I intend being guided in thought, word and deed by my soul.

This intention speaks to the posture of 'beginning surrender' a movement towards allowing more guidance, more of your soul's voice to speak, to reach you.

Conscious action becomes a way of being that develops in different ways for each of us. There is no single prescription.

We thank you for your reading of this piece and feel the energy of intention within it. For some the energy will be, in this moment, more serving than the words.

Blessings.

Power at the Personality Level

At the personality level, power is about being at ease with our personal power instead of denying it and giving it away. Our personal power grows as we develop self-love and spiritual discernment and as we learn our lessons. Our personal power shrinks when we give it away. These are some situations when we give our power away when we:

- feel small in front of another who plays big
- feel intimidated by the speech of another
- hide or bury our voice
- avoid interactions by fear of conflict
- allow decisions to be made for us without partaking in them
- allow others to impose their will on us
- accept deeds which are not aligned with our deeper truth
- allow others to pressure us...

Personal power is a paramount component of the spiritual path. It is not about exerting power, force or control upon us or any other being. This is a misuse of power by the personality self. Personal power comes directly from Source and is the privilege of every oversoul to experience the manifestations of its intentions in the physical/material reality. The gift of free will which is available to every human being implies that one can use personal power in a way which serves one's highest well-being or not; in a way which is in the benefit of all or not; in a way which is aligned with divine will or not.

When we use our personal power out of alignment with divine will, against ourselves or others, we generate chaos in the world.

We lack personal power or give it away to another when we:

- allow someone else to manipulate us
- give more importance/value to someone else's statement or stance than to our own wisdom or intuition

- play ourselves down
- criticise ourselves in favour of someone else
- accept to be silenced
- accept to withdraw
- (accept) to deny our power
- accept what goes against divine will or we go against divine will
- accept what goes against Divine Laws or we go against Divine Laws...

The misuse of personal power and the abuse of someone else's power is at the root of much imbalance in our world:

- Domestic violence and abuse
- Child abuse
- Gender abuse
- Child/adult trafficking
- Prostitution
- Oppression / wars / unrest...
- Political and governmental abuse of human rights
- Psychic attack
- Medical abuse
- Animal abuse.

Whichever form the abuse takes (e.g., physical, psychological, sexual, economic, governmental), there is at the root of it a spiritual power issue which involves taking someone else's power and/or giving one's power away. These are most likely linked to the conclusions of your personality throughout your incarnations.

Remembering that the oversoul has given consent to the experience in your current incarnation is helpful in reclaiming your sovereignty and forgiving yourself and others. Others are not doing something to you: you are the one who has chosen to experience this either out of your conclusions or out of your oversoul's learning plan.

Part of your personal work as an adult and parent is to clear your power related issues and help your child with theirs. As you know now, some conclusions which may have served you well in the past may now be hampering your growth and need updating.

The more of your own personal power issues you resolve, the purer the energy you radiate this enables your child to grow in a healthy environment and master their personal power easier. When parents have unhealthy personal powers, they cannot portray it to their children and enter into power abuse with them as well.

Power at the Soul Level: Divine Will and Power

Effortless, infinite power and peace come from alignment of personal will with divine will. From the perspective of the personality, we cannot understand divine will. Divine will is not something which is to be understood, not even by the oversoul, not even by the monad.

Everything that is (created), has ever been and will ever be stems from divine will. There is a misunderstanding that because we have free will (which we do), we are invited to do whatever we want. The oversoul strives to be aligned with Source for it knows inherently that this is who one is and what serves one's highest well-being. This is best done through the conscious process of aligning personal will with divine will in every divine now moment. It takes humility to do so and at the same time it is a great relief. One can trust in Source and welcome / accept / know / sense / see / feel that one's divine blueprint is ideal for one. As we said, there is tremendous order in the multiverse.

It is a major step and transformation for most people to stop understanding, controlling, debating over right and wrong, good or bad… and instead being surrendered to divine will.

When we talk about this to people, the following question oftentimes arises: do I need to accept everything that happens to me? The atrocities that we are witnessing all over the world, how can they be willed by the Divine?

It is not the place in this book to go into details about why things happen, and we also cannot grasp it fully - as mentioned it is not meant for us to understand. However, the short answer is that indeed just like everything that happens, the Divine wills it. Everything that happens may not be (any longer) in alignment with divine will but the Divine allows it. Asking why is not helpful for no answer can comprehend the truth; asking why only strengthens personality. You can right now decide to let go and be in surrenderedness to what is.

Everything that happens is an opportunity to respond by radiating unconditional love. Especially in the most challenging situations we face, there is the opportunity to transmute fear to unconditional love. When we face any situation within or without us through the eyes of unconditional love, we are exercising free will in the highest possible way we can.

Conclusion

We have introduced the three pillars of parenting in a particular order: limitless power rests on divine wisdom which rests on unconditional love. We are inviting you to anchor your garden of parenting in these three pillars.

As a conclusion to this chapter, we invite you to meditate on this statement:

"The life of every individual is God, and only by the Self-conscious effort to understand life and to express the fullness of good through oneself, can one transcend and eliminate the discords of the outer experience. Life, the individual and the Law are one and so it is unto eternity. This law is

immutable and whatever humankind thinks to the contrary can only cause them to become further lost in matter, creating their things as an outer expression that can only be termed illusion from a Source perspective." [x]

The invitation is to turn your attention to the inner flames of divine love, wisdom and power and let them burn strong for yourself and your children.

PART FOUR: INTENTIONS OF PARENTING (INTENTIONAL-NESS)

Conscious parenting is a journey, just like the project of growing a garden. Depending on where you start, the vision of a lush and vibrant garden may be far away from your present-day situation. From the perspective of Source, there is only this present Now moment. Barbara Ann Brennan says:

"Everything we do rests on the foundation of our intentionality, in the moment we do it. For example, we can say any set of words has a normal meaning, but the way we deliver that set of words can change their meaning drastically. We fill our words with the energy of our feelings and how we deliver those words conveys just what we really intend." [xi]

Working with intentionality is a golden key to conscious parenting and living in general. Before you can experience the garden, you envision in your outer reality, it has to be seeded within you. To experience it in your outer reality, all you need to do is to think and feel it within you with unconditional love and without any restraint. What is in alignment with divine will is your privilege.

In this section, we will explore conscious intention holding and ways that can support your oversoul to build your ideal parenting garden.

Chapter 1
Constellation

Conventionally and especially in the Western world, we have limited our views of Self to the individual aspect. So many of the challenges we face now whether in our personal/family lives or in our social, political, corporate... roles are not allowing for holistic solutions because of this limitation: seeing ourselves as individuals and making the individual the centre of our world-views maintain separation.

We are actually far from being individuals: even at the soul extension level, we are a constellation and always in relationship with the entire universe, whether we are or not aware of it. Understanding that we are constellations is of great help to seek alignment and well-being. When you shift your thinking from individual to constellation, you broaden your perspective on life.

For the sake of simplicity, we will consider in this book that the soul extension corresponds to the individual level (even though we have said already that this is not exactly how it is) and the couple or family is a constellation. What we mean by this is that a couple/family is a group of Source stars, a group of oversouls. It is of great help to the individuals (soul extensions) involved in your family to consciously work with your constellation and the divine light structures that hold it for harmony, balance and well-being.

Divine light structures/constellations have been used by civilisations to accomplish great healing and progress. We are guided to share that this is a revolutionary technology which is not new but has been greatly underused by humanity. It is our privilege to share this technology in this book for a wider use in the benefit of all and for Golden Earth.

What are Divine Light Structures?

Divine Light Structures are the underlying web of light which sustain and structure all of life in the universe. As you have read earlier the example of the frame which holds a rocket together, light structures are what hold a being, a planet, a group consciousness together. Your physicality as a personality is sustained by a human light structure which directly stems from your divine blueprint. There are multiple (infinite) grids that make up creation and we are particularly interested here in the humanity grids. Everything that is willed by the Divine and experienced by human beings are held in the humanity grids.

Every aspect of being human and having a human experience is contained in a grid or light structure. For example, every soul extension has a blood ancestral line and there is for all of humanity an ancestor grid which contains all programs related to ancestors for everyone and all. There is also (multiple) Earth grid(s) which contain all the programs related to planet Earth. Some of these programs are aligned with the divine blueprint while others have been added/

What are Divine Light Structures?

Divine Light Structures are the underlying web of light which sustain and structure all of life in the universe. As you have read earlier the example of the frame which holds a rocket together, light structures are what hold a being, a planet, a group consciousness together. Your physicality as a personality is sustained by a human light structure which directly stems from your divine blueprint. There are multiple (infinite) grids that make up creation and we are particularly interested here in the humanity grids. Everything that is willed by the Divine and experienced by human beings are held in the humanity grids.

Every aspect of being human and having a human experience is contained in a grid or light structure. For example, every soul extension has a blood ancestral line and there is for all of humanity an ancestor grid which contains all programs related to ancestors for everyone and all. There is also (multiple) Earth grid(s) which contain all the programs related to planet Earth. Some of these programs are aligned with the divine blueprint while others have been added/changed throughout the conclusions of the personalities' incarnations.

In this book, we are interested in the grids/light structures when it comes to balancing/harmonising and healing a couple or family from an oversoul perspective.

What do we Mean by Constellation

To explain what we mean by constellation, let us use the example of a family composed of one child and two parents: a mother, a father and a child.

Such a family is a constellation of three soul extensions and oversouls. Because there are three 'stars' involved in this constellation, the ideal light structure which holds this constellation is the 3D triangle - 3 sides (3D personality level) or cylinder - 3 faces (5D soul level). Conscious parenting involves the conscious use of the ideal constellation for the family in their corresponding light structure (here the tetrahedron).

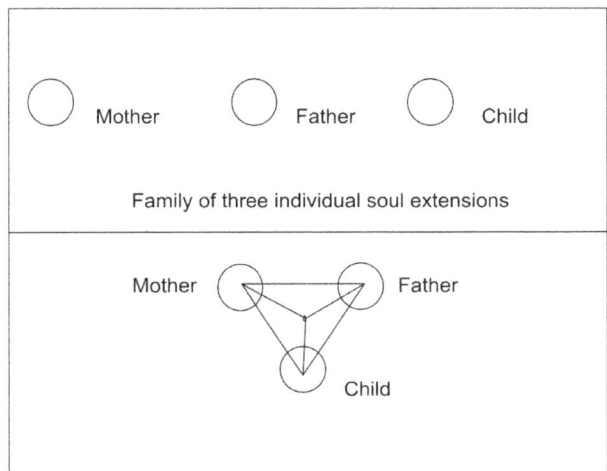

Diagram 15. Example of Family Constellation

Every family (or group) can be held within a divine light structure in an ideal constellation for them. For every family constellation of 2, 3, 4, 5, 6, etc. there is a structure that will support them, a light structure, a geometric shape that will aid them. What is the divine ideal for this?

The 5th density structure is the tetrahedron. There is no requirement for the structure to mimic – in pure geometric terms - the number in the family because this is irrelevant to light structures. The constellation/family will thrive if the family accepts and allows itself to be energetically contained in the light structure which already exists within the infinite universe.

Placing one's family inside the tetrahedron, the pyramid, will align the energetics of the family to the 5th density. It can be a three-sided pyramid or a four-sided pyramid. Or a six-sided pyramid. Or 7-sided. This pyramid structure is infinitely expandable.

Family Constellation Models – Parenting

2 and 3 person family = 3-sided pyramid - in 2D is a triangle

4 person family = Square-based pyramid is also known as a **pentahedron**, 2D is square.

5 person family = 5-sided pyramid – Pentagonal Pyramid. 2D shape is a Pentagon

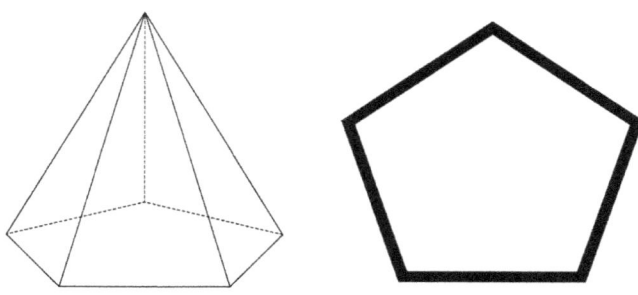

6 person family = 6-sided Pyramid – Hexagonal Pyramid - 2D is a Hexagon

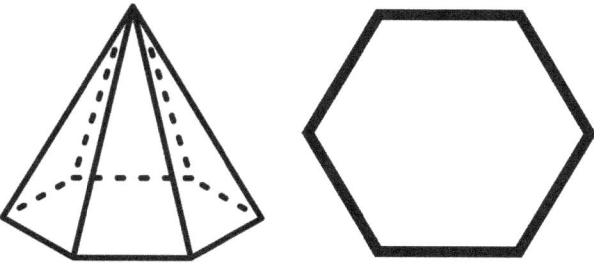

7 person family = 7-sided pyramid - Heptagonal Pyramid - 2D is a Heptagon/Septagon Creative commons.

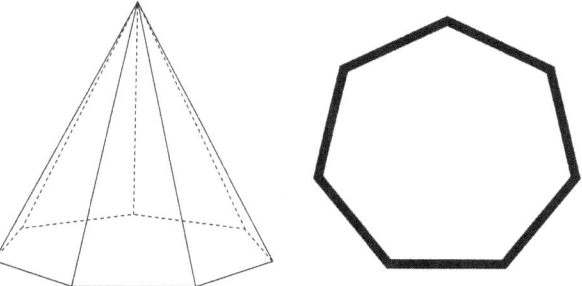

8 person family = 8-sided pyramid – Octagonal Pyramid – 2D shape is an Octagon

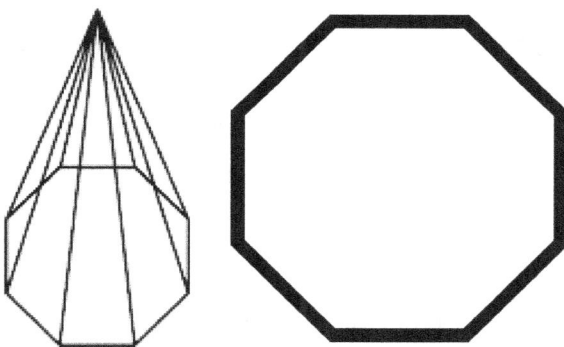

9 person family = 9-sided pyramid – Nonagonal Pyramid – 2D shape is a Nonagon

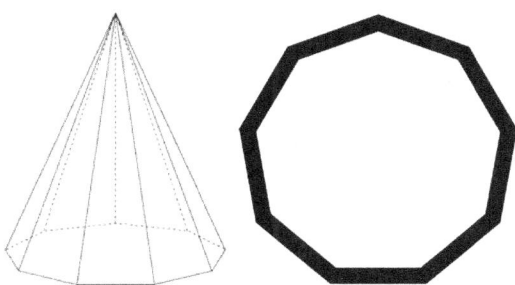

10 person family = 10-sided pyramid – Decagonal Pyramid – 2D shape is a Decagon

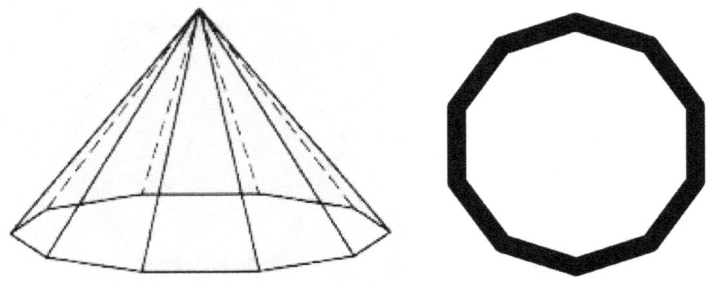

Table 3 - Family Constellations

Number in Family Constellation	3D Shape	2D Shape
2 (include both parents)	3-sided Pyramid	Triangle
3	3-sided Pyramid - Tetrahedron	Triangle
4	Square-base Pyramid	Square
5	Pentagonal Pyramid	Pentagon
6	Hexagonal Pyramid – hexagon base	Hexagon
7	Heptagonal Pyramid – heptagon or septagon base	Heptagon/Septagon
8	An octagonal pyramid is a pyramid with an octagon as its base. An octagonal pyramid has a total of nine faces. The base is an octagon, and it has eight connecting triangles.	Octagon
9	A Nonagonal pyramid. A nine-sided shape is a polygon called a nonagon. It has nine straight sides that meet at nine corners, or vertices.	Nonagon
10	A decagonal pyramid is a solid whose base is a decagon or a ten-sided figure, regular or irregular. The surfaces are ten isosceles triangles, in the case of a regular decagonal pyramid with all the ten vertices meeting at a point.	Decagon

Conversation with Telonis about Family Constellations

The base of the pyramid doesn't really exist... in the sense that it goes to infinity in the light structure. The point at the top of the pyramid may be considered the origin – the creator – Undifferentiated Source. But even this is contrived. This is not really as it is, but it is a useful way to think, conceive it... All are connected to THE ONE. And all are connected to ALL. The point represents the ONE, (ignoring the base) and one are connected to ALL.

The constellation is not a closed structure. It is always connected. The multi-sided tetrahedron represents equal sides of the form – the pyramid and conceiving that its base is open to ALL, the base is not really a base and the pyramid's point, points to the collective origin of the constellation/family which is Undifferentiated Source.

Constellations in the 5th density have the pyramid tetrahedron shape, that is the shape they all have no matter how large the number of faces, the number is infinite, and the size of the constellation is infinite.

It means that the 5th density is one giant tetrahedron. And that would be correct on one level. But it is not an absolute truth.

Everything is determined by Undifferentiated Source.

The 5th density does not only consist of divine light structures in the shape of tetrahedrons. There are many other light structures in the 5th density and there are other building blocks.

There are more than 5 platonic solids. It is not yet released for one to know what those are. All the platonic solids exist in all densities. We say they are building blocks because they are, however, the true building blocks are also infinitesimally small and cannot be discerned by the human eye and not yet by the human scientist – god realised or other – being. The god realised being is not yet able to discern them to any degree of accuracy. The infinitesimally small building blocks of the fabric of the infinite universe are indiscernible to one in this now.

Therefore, we provide a knowable form that one can work with in a real way. The pyramid has immense power within the light structures albeit it is misunderstood in parts. That is less important right now than encouraging souls to interact with the structure. Realise that no matter the size of the structure it is imbued with the same power... the size has no correlation to the power. This has been misunderstood. The small pyramid on one's desk wields the same power as the mighty pyramid if one is unlimited in their beingness and realises it.

What about the experiences people report at the Great Pyramid?

The experiences in the great pyramid happen. That pyramid has been 'primed' for thousands of years and is nurtured and served by many to maintain it as it now is, still a fraction of the power it once commanded. The size is not the issue. The cultivation of the power within the light structure is what we are pointing to... the realisation we wish one to become aware of. In the same way that were a family to cultivate their own 3- or 4- or 5-sided pyramid that would develop a level of power far outweighing its diminutive size.

What of the 2-person family... what shape structure would be divine ideal for them?

This is ideal to ask. Recall we say that the structure is the pyramid.

What about a shape of two intersecting spheres inside a sphere - would that be a useful structure for the 2-person family?

The sphere is a complete closed light structure... closed structures – unified structures have a different signifcance and purpose within the grid architecture - within the structures of light.

The pyramid is still the ideal structure. The two-person family will be constellating with a third person, the child has two parents and both parents are in the constellation. This is so whether the second parent is energetically connected /present / active in the constellation or not.

If one parent is a donor parent, they are part of the constellation energetically.

There is an energetic recognition that regardless of the context the energy of both parents exists within that family constellation... everyone is energetically connected and the pyramid in energetic and light structure terms conveys that perfectly in this now moment.

The pyramid structure is ideal. In this now the pyramid is the structure for constellations of all types, family, corporate and all.

When you work with family members in the divine light structure ideal to them, you can work within the constellation to harmonise and balance all individually and in their relationship to one another. There is no coincidence that a family comes together: the soul extensions are tasked to work together, in this case as a family. For every group of people being meant to work together, there is a constellation.

Constellations are particularly relevant for spiritual growth and integration. Constellations, patterns of 'stars', have extremely powerful energetics.

It may be useful to buy a toy model, or a crystal sculpture, of your ideal constellation and place it in the living room or common space for everyone to see and play with. You can experiment with its energy and notice what happens.

Parenting Through Constellations

Working consciously with constellations as a conscious parenting tool will tremendously help your family life and your couple interactions. Constellations create the ideal spaciousness and attunement for each soul extension / oversoul in the family to ideally progress on their own path but also support one another.

For parents, working with constellations is particularly helpful for several reasons:
- Let's take the example that you and your partner are not part of the same oversoul (which is highly likely) and neither are your children (also very likely): alignment and moderation may be required to put you all in harmony.
- Let's take the example that the entire family belongs to the same group monad, it is however likely that your level of growth and integration (initiation mastery) is not the same, creating discrepancies in your lived experiences and potentially gaps in the way you are drawn to parent your child. This can also generate friction between both parents.
- In general, your child belongs to either your or your partner's monad or group monad. Consequently, there is a natural connection/recognition by the child with the parent who is in the same monad / group monad. You simply are vibrating in the same set of scales and consequently you seem to naturally understand each better (when you are integrated) or on the contrary have strong friction due to multiple unprocessed past lives spent together; you are also likely sharing the same world views/polarities and challenges (at the group monadic level, you are working with the same spiritual challenges). This can create great tension in your lived experiences.
- Parents who have children together at this time are highly likely to have also spent multiple incarnations together in different roles - some of them still unprocessed and painful. Consequently, part of your personality baggage involves your partner, and this is likely to generate friction at the personality level. These are just examples but complex challenges to address and the ideal constellation for your family can help you with them. Constellations are truly amazing light technologies.

When you become aware of such challenges described above, you can consciously place the family members in the corresponding light structure in an ideal constellation and call on support in this light structure. The basic step you can take is to request pure Source light to fill up the constellation. You can also place each member in the constellation and radiate unconditional love to all. You can request alignment, harmonisation, healing, protection... in and for the constellation.

All light structure constellations recommended for families in this book are enhancer and healer structures towards the Golden Earth. We invite you to simply try for yourself and your entire family (parental partner and children): ask for each oversoul to be ideally placed and for the ideal light to fill up the light structure in alignment with divine will and observe the impact. We are guided to recommend filling up your family constellation with aqua blue light, like a waterfall coming directly from source for purification and integration. This is the generic ideal light for all.

Harmonising Sibling Interactions Through Constellations

When you have more than one child, this topic is of relevance in your family. At the soul level, your children have agreed to their order of birth in your family. However, at the personality level, the arrival of a second child often requires a conscious balancing and harmonisation. Unprocessed sibling disharmony can carry throughout adulthood, and it is of great help to your children to consider the exercises for this topic in the *Sourceness Journal*.

It is ideal to place your two children from the moment of conception onwards in the ideal divine structure/constellation for your family and request it to heal and harmonise the links and bonds between all the soul extensions involved.

Some programs pertain to your child/children's spiritual path, and it may not be for you to clear or update them. For example, a child may have as part of their spiritual path in this incarnation to explore jealousy and in this case, it is wise to allow them to do so while being in unconditional love and showing them what unconditional love is in the situations they explore. Other programs are simply leftovers of previous incarnations which are not serving your child/children in this lifetime and as a parent, it is your responsibility to clear them.

One common issue is the non-acceptance of their order of birth: the personality focuses on the limitations of being a 'number 1' or a 'number 2'... If you have two children or more, you are most certainly familiar with this topic. Placing your children in the ideal constellation and calling on balancing/healing light, will help them process the limitations of their personality. We highly recommend a daily practice of calling on the ideal constellation for your family and requesting balance and harmony - this is something you can do together as a family.

Another topic related to sibling interaction is the case of non-incarnated siblings. You may have only one child, but during this or previous pregnancy, another soul was conceived into being without passing the physical birth gate. In this case, your child does have a sibling or twin sister/brother 'in the light'. As an adult you may yourself have a sibling 'in the light'. As you begin working with your family constellation, one of the first requests you can make is to heal and clear any energy cords with all siblings, both incarnated and non-incarnated, that are not ideal for your family. It may be useful to consciously say goodbye to this sibling and free your bonds of any attachment. Healing may be required in this step.

Conclusion

Constellations is a vast topic, and we have covered a basic introduction to experiment with at this stage. The Sourceness Series Book Two and Three are dedicated to constellations: constellations become centre stage as one completes the soul merge. Your basis of operation is no longer individual, but collective and the ground tool for collective work is constellation. Constellations are quite complex and operate multi-dimensionally, multi-level and we are not guided to go in more detail about them in this book. The invitation is to build awareness of being (in) a constellation, to experiment with the structure for your family and notice what happens when you do the suggested exercises.

Chapter 2
Cultivating

Cultivating Subtle Senses

We have introduced the subtle senses in Part One: Chapter 2 (see page 61):
- Clairvoyance
- Clairaudience
- Clairsentience
- Claircognizance

In this chapter, we will go deeper and help you develop these subtle senses. But let's first give you an overview of why it is so relevant to your spiritual and parenting path.

Why Does it Matter to Develop the Subtle Senses?

Developing your subtle senses is foundational to access the soul level. Light is of a finer frequency than the dense physical matter on Earth. The subtle senses are the communication tool of the oversoul, made of light with us. It is simply how the oversoul contacts and guides us, at least at this stage of our evolution.

Like learning a new language, it needs attention and practice, and when you are guided to do so and when you begin to show interest, it is within your reach.

As a parent, developing your subtle senses is of great help when it comes to communicating with your child. Many of the challenges your child is facing cannot be comprehended otherwise. You may have experienced a situation where none of the available information, expert advice, medical recommendation, family wisdom etc... has been useful. We recommend that you experiment with intuited information from your child's team in Spirit and discover for yourself how accurate and helpful these can be. You don't have to be masterful at working with subtle senses to begin receiving relevant and helpful information. What is paramount is the purity of your intention, your centredness in the oversoul and the clarity of your request (we also invite you to read the section on prayer in the foundation of this book).

The Control Panel and the Analogy of the Radio System

As science has shown us, Light is both waves and particles. Waves operate at various wavelengths which is what distinguishes one from another and all are on a continuum. When you tune into a specific radio frequency you get the program of that radio station; when you move the dial, you access another station (which is on a different frequency).

Subtle senses operate much like a radio station: you can tune in and out of them. Thoughts also operate on a certain frequency and likewise you turn their noise off with practice.

You have within you a control panel of your oversoul's 'radio station' which makes it easier to develop the 'clair' skills and communicate with your team in Spirit. You will find in the *Sourceness Journal* exercises to work with your subtle senses control panel and develop them.

Adjusting Your Expectations

When we begin to develop our subtle senses, we can be judgemental about ourselves, impatient and self-deceiving ("I am not doing this right"; "It's not working"; "I will never get this...").

This is a path of self-learning and unlike when you take tests at school, "the right answer" is not written at the end. At the same time, there is an immediate feedback mechanism: at any given point in time, either you get it or you don't. In this sense, it is quite binary: whether you received the information, or you didn't. Such an ability is a muscle that needs to be built and maintained, just like any other muscle.

Patience in this matter is of great virtue. Know that your Guides always look upon you with great encouragement and never judgement. Their patience is infinite.

We invite you to consider this when you judge yourself in any negative manner, even when you think it is justified - for it never is.

Expectations pertain to the domain of personality. The oversoul and your spiritual team do not have any expectations of you. God doesn't have any expectation, only infinite patience, keeping on calling you back to the Light. Expectations have no place in your practice of developing your subtle senses and becoming a clear channel to your oversoul.

Spiritual Discernment is a muscle we have already highlighted, and it is foundational in working with subtle senses. You cannot receive pure information if you are the slightest bit biased in your discernment. Please read the dedicated section on this point in the foundation part of this book.

A Word About Claircognizant Children and Challenges Incurred

Claircognizant children, just like other highly sensitive children, are exposed to a lot of information which their system must digest.

Claircognizant children face an oversaturation of their nervous system: the discrepancy generated by conflicting data between what they perceive and how their environment behaves or reacts to the same information (which it likely does not sense) can create a bug in their information processing. This is even more emphasised by unconscious claircognizance where the child knows without exactly knowing what it knows and why it knows it. As a result, the child can have temper tantrums, anger bursts, illogical behaviours, aggressivity surges... which may seem completely off to the parent, when in fact, the child is having an internal conflict.

A Word About Claircognizant Children and Challenges Incurred

Consider the amount of information a child must process each day and the number of occurrences when it is likely to meet a discrepancy. Can you get a sense of how challenging it can be for a child to have this skill? The gift of a claircognizant child in a family is their very fine **truth telling and outstanding manipulation spotting.** They will challenge you greatly to look at yourselves in refined details and it is truly a precious gift when you see it as such.

To hone this skill, claircognizant children need your support:

- Parents need to give space to their children to live their claircognizance and learn from it to grow their own spiritual discernment and make sense of the information they perceive.
- While giving space to the child to explore their claircognizance and allowing it to inform them, we invite parents not to take everything they hear as either "right" or "wrong". It's simply in formation to work with. It is important not to infuse doubt in the child or themselves, but rather see claircognizance as a communication tool of the oversoul which doesn't work at the personality level. In most cases, you don't even need to react as a parent, but rather allow the child to express and process themselves.
- Parents can learn a lot about themselves from their children and hold impeccable firmness while staying unconditionally loving. For example: claircognizance enables a child to know where a parent is permissive and play this to their favour, by getting them to accept things they normally wouldn't. This can become a limiting pattern in your family constellation. With a claircognizant child, every unexamined aspect of your parenting is under scrutiny, and this is really a great gift. If you are a parent to a claircognizant child it is also likely that your own spiritual path requires the finesse of a high level of spiritual discernment and if that is the case, be sure that you are also equipped and will receive the needed support to hone this.

The resolution here is to refine your personal work as a parent and to guide your child to recognize, accept and use their subtle senses.

What if my Subtle Senses do not Work?

If your practice of developing your subtle senses is not showing results, it may be that you need more time, but it can also be that something else is in the way.

The following lists some of the reasons why our subtle senses may not work:

- Our senses have been manipulated and are dysfunctional.
- We may have unconsciously blocked them by saying things like 'I can't take it anymore' or 'I don't want to hear that', 'I'm tired of feeling xyz'.
- We have shut them down or covered them - out of fear, disbelief, desire to fit in...
- The light structure sustaining them is impaired, damaged, wounded...
- Energetic devices are in place that create dysfunction.

- Spells and enchantments are blocking.
- Veils are covering them.
- Fear is blocking their ideal functioning.
- Energy cords are blocking them.
- Beliefs and Programs are in place which block them.

All these would prevent your ability to tune in and use your subtle senses even if you tried. Your children may also have such blockages.

To address the above, clearing and repatterning are needed. This is not a straightforward process and there are likely multiple layers to work with:

- Your beliefs about Clairvoyance / audience / sentience / cognizance and yourself may have to be carefully examined.
- You may have created (and not be aware of) vows, contracts, agreements, loyalties, decrees, that are binding you.
- There may be learnings which you have not yet attained, which are needed for you to access the subtle senses.
- There may be spells you are not aware of...

The foundational clearing process we offer in this book (see page 162) is a first step in removing anything which is not serving you. There may be more exploration needed and this is also part of building your relationship with your subtle senses.

Cultivating Divine Qualities

When you operate from the personality level, you are not able to hear the voice of your oversoul, nor the guidance from your team in Spirit. It is as if you are completely unaware of their presence. For most people, the journey to the oversoul begins with a leap of faith and a more or less palpable inner knowing or intuition that a personality-led life is like crawling when you are meant to walk. There is no need to judge the personality for it serves the purpose of helping you function in your life until you are ready to upgrade to the oversoul level. Crawling is also a necessary stage.

That transition has been very painful for many people, but now, tools are available to help you make this shift easier. What has been called the 'dark night of the soul' and described as a painstaking stage of wandering and suffering is no longer a necessity.

In the process of transition, divine qualities of the oversoul are here to support you to pave the path. This is the purpose of this chapter.

As you cultivate these qualities, you are bringing them forth into your life, prompting the subconscious mind to believe in a new reality which serves your highest well-being. This process will contribute to updating the non-serving conclusions you carry in your personality by drawing a new reality to you. The richer the prompting, the fuller the experience. Here are some ways you can cultivate a divine quality:

- Saying a mantra out loud: the use of sounded words creates a resonance in your body structure. For example: "I am anchored in divine Trust". Mantras are invocations and we invite you to read again the box "A Word about Working with Invocations" (see page 59).
- Visualising the quality state: the subconscious mind processes reality through images and visual impressions; as you feed it with visualisations of divine qualities, it eases the acceptance process. Gradually, old disempowering images are replaced with empowering ones. For example: see your whole being bathing in divine light, surrendered to the highest Trust.
- Sensing /feeling into the quality: tuning into the quality with your senses and feeling it amplifies the experience you are drawing to yourself. For example: as you see yourself bathing in divine light, feel Trust in every cell of your body. When a thought is charged with emotion it is more powerful.

All divine qualities are seeded within you and therefore are available and within reach. With the intention to cultivate them and regular practice, they will grow. Please be sure of this.

We do not recommend that you "fake it till you make it". This is misleading in our opinion because it manipulates your experience and creates denial within you. When you say any mantra out loud, feel the response of your body to it. By body, we mean the four lower body system which nests your personality. You will find exercises in the *Sourceness Journal* to work with this aspect.

The more you can tune into yourself, the clearer the message of your bodies will appear to you. Listening, sensing, feeling, hearing, watching and observing what is going on within you as you offer a new input to yourself, trains your conscious awareness and your experience of yourself. As you learn this skill, it also becomes available to you when it comes to observing your child. Observation is a divine quality to practice.

Practising with divine qualities is a daily process: repeat the mantra daily as many times as you can remember to, and at least once a day, sit with yourself to observe the impact of saying the mantra to yourself and out loud. You may want to take notes of what you observe as it will give you indications about your blockages and evolution.

It will take a daily practice of a few weeks to grow a divine quality, and of course, it can be longer or shorter. As mentioned, some qualities may take up to a lifetime and more to mature into mastery. To accompany you in developing divine qualities, you will find exercises related to this chapter in the *Sourceness Journal*.

Sourceness: A Series for Golden Earth Being

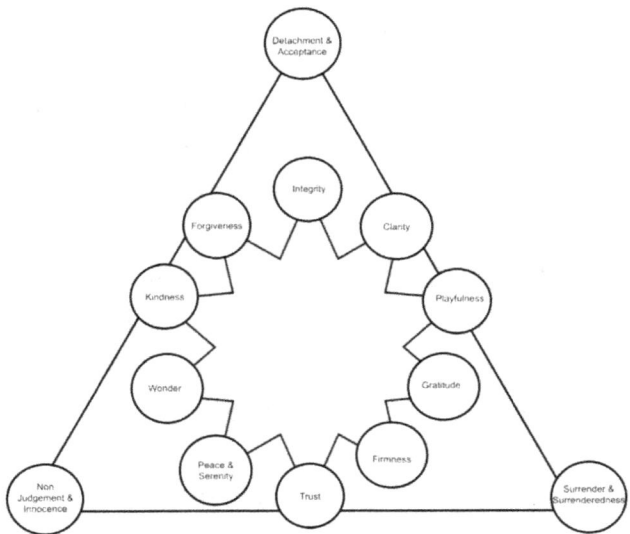

Diagram 16. Qualities of Parenting

1. Non-judgement & innocence

At the personality level

You already know that detached observation is a foundational quality of parenting. Children who are given the space to discover their surroundings in their own rhythm display natural observation. It stems from an inner curiosity and interest in what makes up their environment. When children are educated into belief systems, they gradually lose their natural sense of observation to follow the expectations of the external world coming from parents, school and the mass consciousness they are part of. Their reality is conditioned and shrinks into what is acceptable and accepted, excluding and judging what is not.

As an adult, when you seek to develop the quality of observation you are reclaiming your inner right to experience reality directly, uncensored and just as it is. The more programming you have taken on, the more difficult the re-awakening of natural detached observation. There are two other components to observation: non-judgement and innocence.

Let's look at non-judgement: the subconscious mind, also often called the Thinker, is judgemental by nature. It thinks and categorises, screening according to its inner programs the reality you experience. For example, if in your belief system people are made of a physical body, then it will discard the possibility of seeing their aura, which is energetic. When you would meet a person who can see auras, you may judge them as "weird" or "different" or "crazy" … depending on what your program says. Possibly it may stir you and trigger a 'fault'/rejection mechanism: "it cannot be"; "it's just an exception"; "It's a mistake" … As a result, you may decide to 'discard' the experience, or you may integrate the possibility of a doubt in your belief system. Repeated exposure to events that contradict your inner program, may set you to reconsider your belief system. This is how conclusions in the personality are updated.

Non-judgement is the ability to not judge at all and this doesn't happen at the personality level, which is wired to judge. Instead, to practise non-judgement or non-judgemental observation, we need to suspend the judgemental processes of the subconscious mind. This requires the ability to observe with detachment what is going on in the subconscious mind. Hence the recommendation to create a practice of meditation (see dedicated section in Parent Light Path and Practice Chapter).

Antoine de Saint Exupery wrote "It is only with the heart that one can see rightly; the essential is not visible to the eyes",[xii] suggesting that there is another truth beyond what the mind can grasp. Cultivating non-judgement is about transcending the Thinker. It is a process of dis-identification from the subconscious mind, and opening to experience life as it is being offered to you without trying to label, categorise, dissect, compare or analyse it.

When you can observe without any judgement, you can have a direct experience of life. When you observe your child in this way, you no longer project your own personality's world onto them and give them the space to explore life freely and unconstrained as they truly are.

"If useless thoughts don't cloud your mind, every day is the best day of your life." Zen saying

---

Detached non-judgemental observation is also innocent. Innocence is another quality of non-judgement. This is a spiritual quality. You might remember from your own experience how before you were told that something was "not acceptable" you had not labelled it as such. You were innocent about it. Children are taught that picking their nose or burping in public are "not acceptable" behaviours. But until then, they were innocent about it. When you apply that quality of innocence to the judgements you hold within you, it becomes easier to detach and dis-identify yourself from them. Innocence helps loosen the grip of the subconscious mind. It helps to question and open a space of not-knowing. The program in you says, "it's the way it's done, we have always done it this way' and innocence asks, 'why not look at it differently?'".

At the soul level

While at the personality level you apply effort to suspend judgement, at the soul level detached, non-judgemental and innocent observation is natural. Divine observation is also infused with divine love and light. As you observe at this level - yourself, child or life - you are aware of God's loving presence and light all around you and within you and your child. Everything is an expression of the divine and at the soul level you choose not to resonate with the lower expressions of personality. It is as if you could see / sense / feel / know the soul behind the personality expression, behind the cloud of programs and beliefs expressing themselves.

At the personality level, cultivating observation is about becoming aware of what gets in the way of divine observation. At the soul level, it is about being surrendered to God's divine Love and Light.

When it is missing

The lack of detached, non-judgemental and innocent observation blocks your ability to live and parent consciously; you are at the mercy of the worldviews / beliefs / programs... that have been encrypted in you throughout all your incarnations, some of which are not even yours and you may not even realise it. The process of becoming a conscious adult and parent involves developing these observation skills.

When you judge events and situations through the automatic filter of your subconscious mind you are trapped in the personality. When we are in a judgemental posture, we give ourselves the right to judge, thinking that we are, know, feel, understand, sense... better than others. We discard others by condemning what we judge. All judgement creates separation even those we (at the personality level) may see as helpful because they hold our value system.

Here are some examples of judgements we may think are helpful:
- Judging against violence / war / human rights violation / political oppression...
- Judging against political parties
- Judging against behaviours / attitudes / mindsets
- Judging against clothing styles and looks
- Judging against lifestyles/music choices...
- Judging against the darkness...

We all hold some judgement in our being and we usually believe that as some things are worth dying for, it speaks to our nobility to stand against those who trespass our core values or humanity and judge them. These are personality traps which block us from accessing our oversoul.

As we examine carefully, non-judgement creates healing. Non-judging doesn't mean that we allow anything to happen to us or our child. There is tremendous power in a detached, non-judgemental and innocent "NO" (Please also read the section on personal power for more about this).

2. Detachment & Acceptance

At the personality level

Now that we have talked about detached, non-judgemental and innocent observation. Let's investigate the qualities of detachment and acceptance.

Detachment or non-attachment is a core divine quality that accompanies you on your path as an individual and as a parent. It is the quality of being fully in life without being stuck to any aspect of it. When your child has a want, she will be attached when she doesn't get it. The attachment is expressed in a spectrum between a mild upset and full-blown tantrum. How do you handle such a situation? You may offer something else to distract attention or say "yes but not now; you have to wait a bit"; or help her soothe herself by normalising the situation "it's alright; what you are feeling now is ok and you can't have it. That's fine. Take a breath or go be with your Teddy for a moment…", or any other way. The child will learn to get over the threshold of upset and return to stable peace. This is the process of learning detachment and acceptance of what is.

Every grab, every desire, every wish is an opportunity to practise. Being in non-attachment doesn't mean that we don't care or are indifferent. On the contrary: we care and yet, we are not attached to outcomes. For example, a couple who practises non-attachment may say: "We really would like to become parents! Learning that a pregnancy is underway would be fabulous and we are also ok if it doesn't happen". Non-attachment does not cancel the preference we may have for things, events, situations, relationships, people.

Non-attachment comes in to help us make our choices and let go of what is not in our control. The personality is attached to what it desires, and it takes conscious practice to manage it so that it doesn't impose its wants on us. As we do so, we prepare the personality for greater spirituality in our life. Mastery over the personality involves taming the four lower bodies' wants and desires by practising non-attachment.

As you observe the grabs that get in your way of growing non-attachment, you become familiar with your limiting beliefs, the pulls and wants of your lower mind, the automatic programs and your inner hurdles whether yours or inherited, from this or other lifetimes. As you are in detachment, you can also be in acceptance of what is. And when what you accept, because it is what it is, is not ideal for you, then you can begin looking within and change your inner reality.

At the soul level

The oversoul is naturally non-attached. Acceptance is the spiritual quality of agreeing with what is, because at the soul level there is inner knowing that everything is willed by the divine. Acceptance is a quality of receiving what God/Source is offering us, even if we don't understand it, don't want it, or don't like it. Even when we are dealing with our negative karma and experience events or conditions that are not in alignment with divine will and not for our highest well-being, acceptance helps us process them by being with what is - which doesn't mean that we don't heal or clear the blockage. On the contrary, it helps us step back and observe the situation through the lens of detached, non-judgemental, innocent observation. Then we can deal with what is, and if that is dissonant or out of alignment with divine will, then we can heal and clear it.

Taking the previous example of the couple who wishes to become parents, acceptance is welcoming whatever situation they face in their pregnancy quest by receiving it without moving away from what is nor towards it. They may not become parents if the divine doesn't will it and they may realise that this is so and be at peace with it; or they may realise that something else which they had not yet seen is in their way and decide to deal with it. As they practise detached, non-judgemental, innocent observation and acceptance, they deal with the evolution of their situation as it arises without carrying their past burden into the future or stepping away from the present now into a fantasised future.

When it is missing

In the absence of non-attachment and acceptance we are carried into drama. Here is the typical way a drama takes over in our life:

1) **Trigger:** something happens in the form of an event, an encounter, an exchange or even simply a thought we grasp. For example: you come home tired from a busy day at work and the way your spouse looks at you, displeases you. They don't greet you as you would have wished, and you get triggered.

2) **Activation of the inner limitation:** these are usually limiting beliefs / energetic threads /programs that lie dormant within us until they are triggered by a situation which calls them forth. To continue the example: you interpret the looks of your spouse as a confirmation of the belief/program you hold within you that "nobody cares about you" or "you work so hard, and it's not even appreciated".

3) **Hi-jack of the conscious mind:** when the limitation is activated, it plays its script. It's like pushing on a button and it does what it is programmed to do. Limitations are fascinating in their range of forms, intensities, actions... but they come down to one thing: they steal your freedom to operate.

4) **Acting out / boiling in:** what usually happens when you are experiencing the active limitation is an acting out of the narrative within which displays a drama, or it is suppressed and piles up within you. In our example, you may become grumpy when you catch 'the look' of your spouse and might attack him by criticising him, kicking off a fight, complaining or withdrawing... Your reaction to the trigger is part of your personality-learnt script / coping strategy. There are patterns which you are certainly familiar with as they are your personality's preferred paths.

5) **Stabilisation:** at some point, the tension will cool off and you will return to your 'normal baseline'. In all these steps, the limitation does not get cleared, it simply turns on and off.

A Word on Drama

If you are operating from the disempowering-ego personality level, you are choosing to live in drama. In his works on the drama triangle, Steven Karpman identified three positions which make up all the human postures we take in the stories we live. He called it the Drama Triangle because it is a closed loop:

- **The Victim:** is not owning their willpower and lives at the expense of others. Through a lack of willpower and/or self-love, the victim opens to abuse, mistreatment, punishment... Victim consciousness is a widespread ailment that needs clearing.
- **The Hero:** is responding to the loss of willpower by defending the victim. It is a form of non- acceptance and overtaking of responsibility. Although the hero is portrayed in our human folklore as the "one defending good against evil", it remains a disempowering posture and perpetrates the drama. Hero-ing is a major spiritual trap.
- **The Perpetrator:** is overpowering the victim, aggrandizing oneself. They are often portrayed as the "evil" or "bad guy". The perpetrator needs a victim to overpower - if the victim doesn't deny their own power, there cannot be victimisation.

Our societies, movies and stories are built on the defence of the "poor victim" against the "evil perpetrator", glorifying the Hero, justifying war and violence in the name of freedom and moral values. However, there is no freedom within the drama triangle - neither in the relationships between postures, nor in the posture itself.

All three postures are a disempowering personality expression and need each other's power wound to operate. At the heart of all human drama lies the identification with victim consciousness and the original wound of separation and disempowerment. The moment one recognizes one's own divine nature, exit from the drama triangle becomes possible. It is the personality that gets trapped in drama, not the oversoul.

There is a simple healing key to the drama triangle: as a light structure, the triangle is a healing. When you are caught in a drama triangle, if you go in the centre of the triangle and request healing, you will find that the grip the positions hold over you will loosen. It is like going in the eye of a storm, the middle point where all is calm.

3. Surrender and Surrendered-ness

At the personality level

At the personality level, you practise surrender by releasing control, perfectionism and tightness in the four bodies: you allow for energy to flow, for events to unfold, for your emotions to be felt, your thoughts to float by, the world to express itself around you and through you. You want to no longer resist what is.

To link it back to the previous qualities we have introduced, It is surrender that enables detachment and acceptance. At the personality level surrender is an action: the personality does not surrender, so it requires our conscious intention and effort. Like with suspending judgement; in order to surrender, we need to suspend control.

At the soul level

Here, we are no longer exerting effort, we are surrendered. We talk about surrendered-ness: it is the experience of being surrendered as a state of being. Surrendered-ness is the present-ness state or beingness of surrender.

In surrendered-ness we are not opposing any resistance, any control nor grab: we are in this state of being surrendered. In surrenderedness there is no longer any action, just a quality of being, receiving Love with Love, Light with Light. At the soul level, you practise surrendered-ness by being the Love and the Light you are. You are no longer resisting because there is nothing to resist. Everything in your life is a gift for you to experience, to learn, to grow, to evolve, to express who you are in every divine Now moment and communicate with others. At the soul level, everything is an expression of the Divine Unity which you are.

Especially when things get tight in you because your experience is not one you like or are comfortable with, or when you are surrounded or overwhelmed by energies whose vibrations are not ideal for you, calling on the quality of surrendered-ness helps you accept what is and create a spaciousness within you to deal with the situation from a place of love and power. It doesn't mean that you are denying or suppressing it, but rather welcome it so you can transform, transmute, heal or clear it.

When you are practising to create the bridge from personality to soul, it is recommended to cultivate the being quality of surrendered-ness.

A Word About 'Surrenderedness' and Other 'ness'es

Why do we use the word surrenderedness?

We may be very familiar with the concept of surrendering to God, or Source. It has been pointed out to us that linguistically there are issues with the following words:

Surrender - present tense

Surrendering - present continuous

Surrendered - present perfect

These are all attached to 'time' in grammatical terms. The issue according to our guidance is that our words don't convey a state of being in the way that might be helpful when we are in a different consciousness.

So adding 'ness' to words indicates that we are referring to a present / now / current state of beingness.

When it is missing

The opposite of 'surrenderedness' is control. We are holding tight on to life because we cannot trust that we are safe, cared for, supported, divine. We don't see the higher meaning of our life and cannot relax into it. Control is a coping strategy of the personality to navigate through the challenges, hardships and risks of life. From the personality standpoint, we do not see that we are the ones creating our reality through our thoughts and feelings; what we put control on becomes tighter, reinforcing our belief that control is necessary.

In the physical body, control activates the sympathetic nervous system, kicking stress in and getting us ready to run and fight through life; while surrenderedness activates the parasympathetic nervous system, bringing about relaxation, flow and spaciousness in our body. It doesn't mean that to be active, we need control: we can be active and surrendered at the same time; we can be fully relaxed and infused with the energy of enthusiasm for what we are doing. When we are surrendered, we widen our capacity to observe what is happening and feel into what is emerging through and with us. Surrenderedness is in this way a quality that supports creativity.

4. Trust

At the personality level

Trust is a foundational quality at both levels of parenting. At the personality level, it is about trust in yourself, your abilities, talents, skills, growth, opportunities; that you belong and are not alone; that you are loved and lovable; that you are powerful, way more than you can imagine; that you can access the answers that you seek within you and find the resources you need to face the challenges of life. It is also about trusting that it is okay to surrender to the unknown and be relaxed in uncertainty, to release the grip of control and the need for knowing or understanding; that it is okay to be without any action.

Trust at the personality level, prepares the grounds for the lower mind to allow the oversoul to take charge. It is very helpful to train the mind to believe that all the help and support you need at any point is available to you as you request it.

For many of you, building trust and preparing the personality / soul extension, to welcome a deep trust in Self and God is a life changing development. It may require bypassing and clear many limitations and blockages in the four lower bodies. The more distrust there is in your personality, the more self-love and patience are needed to reprogram the subconscious mind and release the tightness of the emotional/physical bodies. If you carry within your personality deep issues related to trust / distrust / betrayal, it is highly recommended that you give particular attention to the exercises in the *Sourceness Journal* around this quality.

At the soul level

When you are attuned to the divine quality of Trust at the soul level, you are an embodiment of Trust. You are anchored and rooted, aligned and expressing the quality of trust at a much deeper and infused level than the personality can. There is an inner knowing / sensing / feeling that trust is within you and all around you. The absence of trust is no longer even an option. You are imbued with sourceness, and your divine path is unfolding ahead of you as you take each step. You trust in your divine purpose, in divine Love, Will and Power that you are. You trust in Trust-ness, the experience of being in Trust, but also in Trusted-ness, the experience of being trusted in the present now. That trust is not directed towards a person, it simply is evolving within you, through you, around you as Trust.

When it is missing

The absence of trust is often the result of betrayal and abuse experiences. Every hurtful and painful experience can lead to a lack of trust and affect any of your bodies - not only the four lower ones, but also the spiritual ones.

When distrust is in place, it is always affecting the four lower bodies too: the subconscious mind puts in place programs/beliefs and coping mechanisms to keep the risk of trust misuse at bay. The personality is then driven by fear and becomes closed to the experience of unconditional love. Consequently, it also blocks the possibility of trust and surrenderedness. You may have registered this lack of trust in your physical and etheric body, in your emotional body and/or in your lower mind. Distrust can also affect your spiritual bodies: for example, distrust in God would not only be found in the personality level, but also in the higher bodies.

Distrust can taint your sense of safety - physical and psychological, limit your openness and welcoming of others/relationships; it may also limit the range of experiences you are welcoming in your life, and it can hamper your oversoul's ability to reclaim sovereignty.

On your parenting path, Trust is such a foundational quality and is affecting all aspects of your life and who you are; thus, it requires your utmost care. Also, if you focus your attention on building Trust at the soul level, the personality trust will take care of itself: your oversoul will guide you and all the gaps will surface for you to take care of them.

5. Peace & Serenity

At the personality level

A calm mind, a peaceful emotional body, and a relaxed physical body are signs of a balanced personality. We live in such stressful times with such pressure and demands on the four lower bodies, that it is primordial to keep the personality level in harmony and balance for it to be a stable foundation for the oversoul integration.

Peace and serenity are divine qualities that:
- the lower mind experiences when it is calm and not occupied with fear-based activities,

- the emotional body experiences when it is non-triggered and in love - its natural state,
- the physical/etheric bodies experience when they are healthy.

We recommend you make these qualities foundations in your parenting garden for your own sake and the healthy development of your child. These qualities will not only maintain the healthy harmony of your four lower body system, but they will also help you face the increasing challenges that are arising and will likely continue to arise in this phase of transition Earth and humanity are experiencing:

- An acceleration of the experienced speed of life.
- An increased exposure to stimulation and pollution of all sorts (electronic, electromagnetic, etheric, chemical, emotional, mental…).
- An increase of tension between the forces and polarities at play on Earth and within us, which also increases the confusion and fear levels in and around people.

It is as if the heat is going up on multiple dimensions and spaces of response are tightening, creating an increasing stress and toxicity in the body system, saturating the sympathetic nervous system, and amplifying all the dissonance and fears which are required to surface so they may be cleared.

The stress from your environment and lifestyle is affecting you and rippling negatively on your child. But that stress is also an indicator of inherent tensions within you. Cultivating peace and serenity is highly recommended to all human beings in these times. It is a necessary state to develop to navigate these times masterfully. We highly recommend that you consciously create a cocoon of peace and serenity in your home, and in your life in general, by carefully selecting the exposures and activities you allow for yourself and your child.

At the soul level

To the oversoul, peace and serenity are natural states. All the experiences of the personality are overseen by the oversoul and agreed before incarnation. There is nothing that one experiences that is not either within one's plan or within one's reach of transformation. The oversoul is available upon request to help with any experience or condition that is not, or no longer, aligned with divine will.

At the soul level, when the experience is not one of peace and serenity, you can have curiosity about what is generating dissonance: is this part your learning plan? Is this something that is residual from unresolved or unprocessed past challenges? Through this process of detached observation and inquiry you can address any dissonance and either complete the learning and move on, or clear what's in the way so you may return to the oversoul's natural state of peace and serenity, which is also the emotional body's natural state.

When it is missing

The opposite of peace and serenity is stress, anxiety, distress, divide, agitation… Like blurred waters, the mind loses its natural stillness, and the emotional body is distraught. The personality cannot remain in the present now and is closed to unconditional love: fear takes over. This is an unhealthy state of your four lower bodies which generates imbalance in the lower mind, the emotional body and ultimately ripples down into the physical through illness. There is so much stress and anxiety in our societies, amplified by the media and the socio-economic/political structures that it takes utmost vigilance and the highest levels of conscious work to detach oneself from such levels of dissonance. This terrain is the particular focus of dark forces which, by design, stand against the coming of the Golden Age on Earth which we are all serving. These forces feed on the escalation of human fear for they know that you cannot integrate your oversoul and realise your divine nature as long as you are driven by fear.[xiii] The slightest fear within you can be used to manipulate you and take you off-track. The most effective and only antidote to fear is unconditional love. Please reflect upon this very carefully and as much as you need until you can make this your inner truth: your own health and your children's health ultimately depend upon this realisation. If there is one thing you should give the top priority to and focus on it is this: master unconditional love and commit to peace and serenity over fear in every divine now moment.

You will find in the *Sourceness Journal* many practices to remove all fears from within you and maintain a state of peace and serenity. We also invite you to read the chapter on the pillars of parenting dedicated to love and practice with your Pillar of Light to always maintain the integrity of your energy system.

6.   Wonder

Wonder is a divine quality of the oversoul, a natural quality of the divine child. If you recall a situation when you experienced wonder, you may feel in your body a lightness, your gaze expanding towards the horizon, and an exploratory energy igniting in your heart. Wonder is the energy of exploration, invention, creation… It is not attached nor interested in what is already known or certain, but rather seeks what is beyond. Wonder is a precious quality that accompanies the process of dis-identifying with the personality towards an oversoul led life.

At the personality level

At the personality level, excitement can be disguised as wonder. The insatiable thirst for new experiences, discoveries, explorations without connection to the oversoul. This is a personality trap. To the extreme, excitement can turn into restlessness and the inability to pause and be still. It can become an addiction.

Wonder at the personality level is often related to the archetypal energies of the Pioneer, the Explorer or the Adventurer which infuses the personality with this energy of discovery and curiosity for the unknown. Your conscious work when developing wonder at the personality level is to link to the discovery and exploration of the oversoul. Turning the inquisitiveness and curiosity towards pathing your spiritual way. This requires a level of open-mindedness and flexibility in the personality. If you are reading this book, you probably do not have a fully rigid personality and already feel the call of your oversoul. Wonder is the quality you want to breathe both into the tight places within you to allow for what is ready to crumble and into the pockets of air which are ready to grow your fire stronger. When your personality tightens its grip, you can use wonder to shift your energy towards lightness and spaciousness. When you hear the call of your oversoul, you can use wonder to expand your horizon and follow the "what if?", "I wonder what would happen if I …"

Wonder puts your life into movement towards a different destination than the fixed line your personality is keeping you on, the destination of your oversoul.

At the soul level

Wonder is a core quality of the divine child. It is the awe and marvel towards creation and divine movement/evolution. It is the joyful appreciation of the limitlessness of all the possibilities offered to us within our divine blueprint. Wonder helps us explore our divine power and expand further and beyond with every breath we receive. The expression of wonder is pure joy and unconditional love for life and Source.

When it is missing

Imagine you are taking a walk on the beach on a rainy day and the sand has become mushy. As you walk, your feet sink in but it is possible to continue the walk. Now imagine you are walking in a pool of fresh cement: you may be able to take a few steps, but soon the cement will harden, and you will be caught in it. A life without wonder, is like walking in cement: you are stuck in the worldview of personality, its tight belief system, its automatic programs, rigid assumptions, fears and denials. The challenge for a wonderless personality is that your views of life shrink, and it keeps you secure in what you already know without any windows into the oversoul. Like a self-fulfilling prophecy, beliefs systems you hold in your personality project into your reality and reinforce themselves as your truth which you think is 'the' truth. Statements such as "we have always done it this way" or "it is just how things are" are extreme illustrations of a tight personality led life. Infusing wonder into the personality brings fresh air and movement into your life. Wonder is linked to innocence.

The opposite of wonder is closed mindedness. You are not open to trying anything new be it food or ideas, places or experiences. There is no inquiry or inquisitiveness alive in a sleepy mind. The opposite of wonder is also expectation. When we meet someone, we know and do not see in them anything we have not already seen; when we believe we already know what someone is going to say; when we believe that we already know what is going to happen. And we do not mean here the inner knowing of claircognizance, but rather the automatism of the personality. Inner knowing emerges moment by moment when we are truly aligned with the divine; it is not the result of past knowledge or rigid conclusions. Relationships that are settled in expectation are not allowing new life to infuse them. They do become flat and flavourless. In the absence of wonder, we cannot truly meet someone, and we cannot truly experience the magnificence and marvel of life. It's the routine life, day in and day out; the same old same; the boredom of existence.

Children have a natural inclination for wonder which grows as it is nurtured. Conversely, when it is not valued it becomes dormant and conformity takes over. In the absence of wonder, everyone plays the same games, has the same interests, eats the same food...

7.   Kindness

At the personality level

Kindness is another foundational quality to cultivate in your parenting garden: kindness to yourself, your child, your spouse, people around you - near and far - all beings, the Earth and all there is. Kindness warms the heart and melts judgement, divide and grudge.

The challenge with kindness at the personality level is when it lacks unconditional love: it remains transactional and expects return. The kindness that we are encouraging you to develop and include in your parenting garden is not at the personality level.

At the soul level

At the soul level, kindness is an inherent quality of the oversoul. It is companionship or kinship with others who, like us, are a unique expression of the Divine on their spiritual journey. Kindness is a quality of the divine child. When you are connected to the divine child within you, you can experience natural kindness as your state of being. It is linked to innocence and appreciation/gratitude.

Soul level kindness is not personal and not necessarily directed towards someone; it is divine benevolence expressed in our experience as we choose to tune into it. It doesn't serve a purpose as in "being kind to someone because it's polite" and is not transactional, as in "it's what you do to live respectfully with each other in society". Instead, it is for its own sake. At the soul level, there is an inner knowing / sensing / seeing / feeling that all of creation is One and kindness is the natural inclination one has towards all. At the soul level, everyone is a friend. This reminder is of great help when you face challenges with someone at the personality level.

Souls are kind, benevolent and generous because it is their divine nature. You may have heard or said yourself "he's such a kind soul" or "she's such a beautiful soul" - what this is referring to is the soul shining through and being experienced / visible / knowable / sensed at the personality level; actually, all souls are beautiful, kind, generous, joyful, peaceful…

When we do not experience this, it is because we are operating at the personality level in its negative expression. You can train your personality to be kind, and you can welcome kindness as a quality of who you truly are, at the soul level.

When it is missing

The opposite of kindness is closed heartedness rooted in fear: the heart has gone cold, stiff and closed. In this state, you experience separation and disconnection. If you lack kindness in you it certainly is related to an inner child wound.

8. Forgiveness

Forgiveness is the act of "giving love", Free of Resentment (FOR): FOR-GIVING.

At the personality level

Forgiveness enables us to move forward in our evolutionary experience. The personality will remain stuck with its past conclusions if it chooses not to practise forgiveness. You may have heard people saying, "I will never forgive him" or "this is something I just cannot forgive". These are just expressions of a hurt personality blocked in the pain and not ready to learn from the situation. That personality may stay stuck for a while, for a lifetime or for aeons. When the soul extension is ready to forgive, it can integrate the learnings of that painful experience, amend its conclusions and move on. We have free will. If you choose to withhold your forgiveness, that is your choice. And your choice to continue to experience the emotions and thoughts that go with that.

As human beings, we make mistakes and mistakes enable us to learn and evolve. There is nothing inherently faulty in us and no judgement to have about any of our mistakes. The judgements we hold against ourselves, and others hamper the learning - the remembering of our God-self - as they block our ability to forgive. If we hold a grudge against a situation, someone, ourselves, we are attached and identified. Then when we are ready to forgive - ourselves, others, the situation, God - the flow of love can return within us. Forgiveness sets life into motion and gives a new perspective.

At the soul level

We might restate what forgiveness is in the style of an affirmation or intention:

"Free of resentment, I AM giving unconditional love in this and in every divine now moment".

The very nature of unconditionality is that - it has no conditions. Meaning that in any situation:

- You may not receive or see any external benefit for giving forgiveness - personalities often forgive in the hope of getting some kind of positive strokes for doing so. Forgiveness at the soul level has no expectations.
- You may not fully understand all that you are forgiving, meaning your personality may crave/require to get the 'full picture'. Spiritual forgiveness requires no such understanding… you are in complete surrenderedness with Source that forgiveness is instantly given, even you do not understand and even if your personality disagrees.

When we state forgiveness in this form "Free of resentment, I AM giving unconditional love in this and in every divine now moment", we place our being in an intentional state of present beingness, and so are aligned with divine will, Love, Wisdom and Power.

At the soul level we are first concerned with looking within our own being. Look within first. What emotions are you experiencing?

The mantra we suggest experimenting with is:

"I forgive myself; I forgive all."

When it is missing

The opposite of forgiveness is condemning, blaming, punishing, holding onto grudges and withholding love. Forgiveness can be imagined as an open palm with liquid light resting in it; when the hand is closed and formed into a tight fist, all the light is squeezed out. Forgiveness is the open giving hand filled with the light of unconditional love.

When forgiveness is missing there is often refusal to accept what has happened, what is and the associated feelings. When we refuse to forgive, we block the healing/resolution process. There may also be a reaction to blame the other.

9. Integrity

Integrity is the quality of alignment of the personality with the oversoul. As such, it is a foundational quality and a reference: "am I in integrity?" is a question to ask regularly as a parent on the Light Path.

At the personality level

Integrity at the personality level is when we align our four lower bodies in harmony with one another: what we experience and convey energetically is the same as what we feel and the same as what we think and the same as what we experience in our body.

In his book Soul Psychology, Joshua David Stone offers valuable exercises to balance and harmonise the four lower bodies. This is a reading we highly recommend. You will also find in the *Sourceness Journal* exercise to balance and harmonise the four lower bodies.

At the soul level

Integrity at the soul level is when the four lower bodies are in balance and alignment with each other and in service to the oversoul. The oversoul is thus sovereign, in charge of us and the personality is aligned with the oversoul, surrendered to it and in service to it. Full integrity happens when you complete soul merge.

Integrity at the soul level also means that you are mending and balancing within you the three divine pillars of Love, Wisdom and Power. The practice of nourishing and balancing the three-fold flame in your heart which is described in the *Sourceness Journal* will help you build integrity at the soul level and contain the personality in divine integrity.

When it is missing

Here are some examples of what happens when we are not in integrity:
- We think something and say something else.
- We think something and feel something else.
- Our body signals something and we say something else, deny it or suppress it.
- We feel something and hide it, reject it, negate it.
- We deny or reject the guidance of our oversoul.
- We energetically express something and say something else.

These create chaos in us and consequently in our life. Lack of integrity is misalignment, manipulation, judgement, dishonesty, refusal of the personality to be surrendered to the oversoul, rejection of higher love, wisdom and power.

10. Clarity

Clarity is the quality of being undisturbed by confusion, fog, distress, fear, dissonant emotions, dissonant energies, limiting beliefs or forms, and thus being able to see / know / feel / sense / hear what is as it is. It is like removing dirty glasses and suddenly seeing clearly or removing earplugs and hearing clearly.

At the personality level

Clarity is a resulting state of being in alignment and integrity within yourself. It is not really a quality you can directly cultivate; however, It is possible to invite clarity in your life by holding the intention of experiencing it and by doing your personal work to remove obstructions. Like a polished diamond that shines through and forth, we can experience clarity because it is an expression of the divine nature we are. The work, however, is in the polishing.

It is important to mention that the experience of clarity is so wonderful that it may create an attachment in the mind: we want to get back there. Attachments take us out of the direct experience of the Now - which is all there is. The moment you are attached to something, you are creating a biased and limited reality, blocking the natural flow of life. By having an attachment to clarity, you simply cannot experience clarity.

At the personality level, clarity helps you build discernment: when you ask questions such as "am I in integrity?", or "am I forgiving or am I holding a grudge?" you build clarity.

Developing and experiencing clarity comes down to doing your personal work of aligning and harmonising your four lower bodies; removing blockages and practising the other divine qualities listed in this chapter; as well as intentionally calling on clarity in your life.

At the soul level

Clarity at the soul level is about experiencing the radiance of your oversoul. When you embody the light that you are, in the unique divine radiance of your divine blueprint then you are radiating clarity in and all around you.

As we have mentioned above, clarity is a resulting quality of doing your clearing work and preparing your personality to welcome the oversoul. It is also related to your work with the subtle senses: the more honed and sharper your subtle senses, the greater the clarity of your perception. The clarity we are talking about here is non-conceptual and doesn't have anything to do with thinking or the intellect; it is divine clarity perceived directly by your conscious mind through the subtle senses. With clarity, you can hear God and the Guides speaking to you directly.

When it is missing

Absence of clarity is confusion, fogginess, disconnection, lack of purpose... it is as if your inner compass was out of order. You don't know who you are, what you are doing here, what your life is about.

11. Playfulness

Playfulness is a helpful quality to cultivate in your garden to keep things light and easy going, and also have fun in the process of parenting. While parenting is an important act of service and a great responsibility, it doesn't have to be serious, hard or strenuous. Things get much smoother and enjoyable when playfulness is cultivated by the parents.

At the personality level

Playfulness is a quality of exploration and discovery of one's creativity. It is a quality of the inner child. When you leave children with some items, their inner curiosity kicks in and they will engage in play with them, exploring and discovering what can be done with them, they will taste, smell, move, tap... Children naturally know and understand the language of play.

Playfulness is linked to wonder. There are no limitations to the form that play can take when we do not impose ideas upon it. Playfulness is about dropping external rules and instead following the energy alive in and between us.

Children naturally want to play all the time and getting them to do things which are necessary can also be smoothened through play. This does not mean that everything should be infused with playfulness. It is not always the case that everything is just fun or play. Some things just must be willed, but playfulness comes naturally.

At the soul level

At the soul level, playfulness is a natural quality of the divine child; it is the experience of following the divine energy the oversoul resonates with wherever it takes you in this divine now moment. In play the heart is light, open, joyful, alive, vibrant. When you experience this flow of energy through playfulness, you are in direct connection with your oversoul. The divine child within is inherently moved by the oversoul's vibration and when we allow this flow to move through us without restraining or constraining it, we are in play with life. For this to happen, we need to prepare the personality by removing fears and limiting programs/patterns. Thus, we experience playfulness at the soul level by preparing the personality and consciously reconnecting to our divine child.

When it is missing

The opposite of playfulness is closed mind and heartedness. When playfulness is missing, the personality functions under a tight grip of external conditioning and identifications with rules and fears. When you are not experiencing playfulness, you are disconnected from your divine child and thus your oversoul.

Every time you create an interaction with playfulness you develop your bond with it. You may also consciously make a connection with the energy of playfulness whenever you play with your child or even when you just think about play - this way, you strengthen it daily.

12. Gratitude

Gratitude is the quality of thankfulness and appreciation for what is, for all of creation, whether we understand, experience or agree with it or not.

At the personality level

The quality of gratitude we talk about here is not transactional nor conditional: conventionally you are grateful for something or towards someone for something they have done for you. This is not gratitude. It's a learned behaviour.

What we mean instead is the nurturing of an open heart which allows for love to pour in and out of you. When it comes to parenting, gratitude is the quality which helps you stay tuned to love as you interact with your child, as you face the challenges of parenting, as you go through your day. When there is gratitude, we look at the world through a positive filter which invites more of that vibration into our life. In this sense, gratitude is a catalyst.

Gratitude is also the quality which helps us stay detached from outcomes: whether what you wished for happens or not, you stay in gratitude for divine will has your back and is operating always for the highest benefit of All.

Gratitude helps us develop unconditional love: where there is unconditional love, there is gratitude; and where there is gratitude, unconditional love can thrive. When you nurture gratitude at the personality level, you are creating fertile grounds for the oversoul to radiate through you.

At the soul level

At the soul level, gratitude is the oversoul's response to Source's infinite love. It is the natural response of love towards love. Everything - that is all that we experience, all being, all of Creation - is a gift. When we can recognize this, we are naturally radiating gratitude.

There are many ways to tune to gratitude and one of them is to realise that all the help you need and ask for is available and granted to you on your oversoul journey. There is infinite love, wisdom and power available for you. Your spiritual journey is a wondrous path that leads you to your full experience of your unique expression of Source; and so is your child's spiritual journey. The hierarchy is grateful to you for your dedication to your path and for taking responsibility for the child you are parenting.

When it is missing

The opposite of gratitude is a mindset of deserving: when we think things are owed to us; that life owes us what we have. We become tight and ungrateful for the gifts of our life, taking them for granted and growing a nudge for not having more, for things not being perfect from the standpoint of our limited personality, disconnected from the abundance and ever flowing possibilities of life. The antidote here is to become aware that we have fallen in the grip of limitations and gently release the tightness, attuning ourselves to gratitude.

Likewise, if you hold beliefs that you are not deserving of what life offers you or not worthy of receiving it, you are disconnected from gratitude and limiting yourself.

13. Firmness

Firmness is the quality which enables the parent to love the child unconditionally with a clear stance. Firmness is not about rules, regulations, conditions or rewards, it is the energy which holds an intention unshakable. It is the encouragement behind a yes when a child is seeking parental comfort to dare something new, adventurous or scary. It is the boundary behind a no which does not invite further discussion or negotiation. It is the loving presence which witnesses a child's emotional outburst without pushing it down, away or mellowing it.

Firmness is like a loving structure that embraces the child to help him find his direction; a structure not made of bricks, but loving light which conveys assurance, confidence, trust.

At the personality level

Let's look at the quality of firmness through the challenges we face with it:
- When it is lacking, parents are permissive, and the child lacks the safe boundary she needs to develop herself.
- When it is there but hard, parents are unloving and generate a sense of separation with the child - hard firmness is like conditional love. This suggests that the parent needs developmental and/or healing work.
- When it is too soft, it fails to protect the child by providing the boundaries to the path she is exploring. A consequence of too soft firmness is parent-child negotiation (the child naturally wants to explore boundaries and will stretch the limits to find this safe wall - when it is not strong enough, it will fail to provide the container the child needs). This also suggests the parent needs developmental and/or healing work.
- When it is inconsistent, it creates insecurity for the child in areas where firmness is lacking. Inconsistent firmness is a sign of unexamined parental issues or questions.

Drawing on all the other divine qualities to assist us with the situation at hand helps find ideal firmness in every Divine Now moment. At the personality level, firmness is about personal power. Please read the dedicated chapter to this topic under the Divine Pillars of Parenting.

At the soul level

At the soul level, the quality of firmness is related to Divine Power. When you are held in your Pillar of Light, sealed and protected, you are within a light structure that enables you to connect to Divine Power. When you are aligning your personal free will to divine will, you are connected to Divine Power.

When you are connected to your oversoul, you also know inherently who you are, what you have come to experience and which experiences are not for you, what is aligned with divine will and what is not. There is a quality of firmness to what you say yes and no to. At the soul level, firmness can be subtle and gentle, or it can be strong and loud, and even sometimes destructive of old structures that are not in alignment with divine will.

Working With the 12 Planetary Rays

You and your child's unique vibrations are defined through a set of light rays in your and your child's oversoul and monadic templates. Every oversoul, every monad is composed of all rays, but the ideal expression and balance of rays is unique to each oversoul/monad throughout all of its incarnations.

There are infinite numbers of rays; however, to this date, we have been given 12 to work with consciously by activating, balancing and integrating them in our body system.

Working with the rays is an amazing light technology for you as an adult and for your child, and also for the constellation that your family makes.

What are the 12 Planetary Rays?

The 12 Planetary Rays were introduced to us through the works of Alice Bailey between 1919-1949. Alice Bailey initially introduced 7 rays to work with and in recent years another 5 Rays were made available to us.

Our guides mention that the Planetary Rays are vast in their expression. They have identified that it may be helpful at this time to note how each Ray is expressing itself in this now.

Our guides also note that Ray expression changes. It is not the same now as it was in Alice Bailey time. It has also changed since Summit Lighthouse published its version.

Table 4 - The Rays' Expression Changes

RAY		Now
1	Will or Power	Divine Power, Will and Mission
2	Love or Wisdom	Divine Wisdom
3	Active Intelligence	Divine Light Technology and Science
4	Harmony through Conflict	Divine Peace and Harmony
5	Concrete knowledge or science	Divine Pattern Science at Group/Cosmic level

| 6 | Devotion or abstract idealism | Divine Ideal |
| 7 | "Organisation and Ritual" or "Ceremonial organization" or "Ceremonial Magic or Order" | Divine Transmutation |

Clarification Questions on Divine Love

Channelled Message from Melchizedek, Universal Logos.

Question: I am that I am is in intendingness ask for clarity as to why divine love is not mentioned in the above table, as is ideal and in divine will.

Channel is open.

M: Greetings, beloved.

One is Melchizedek. One responds to one asking for clarity.

Divine love has been misunderstood by humanity for some time... one does not judge that this is so, one observes that there is confusion.

ALL knows no bounds, ALL is bountiful.

Divine love is ALL THAT IS and ALL THAT IS is divine love.

There is no more to say. There is nothing to quantify or describe. One can feel / sense / know / hear divine love. Accept that this is so.

Question: One does accept this. Is one saying that divine love is not a Ray in the way the other rays are described?

M: Yes. This is exactly what one is saying. When the first information came in about Ray 2 it was denoted as love or wisdom. It is not love – Ray 2 is divine wisdom.

Question: Thank you, that is clear. Is there anything else that one requires for clarity on this topic?

M: Love as the all-pervading isness of Source is ineffable – meaning too great or extreme to be expressed or described in words – meaning to cause too much emotion that cannot be described– inexpressible in

words. To seek to describe that which cannot be described does not align with mastery.

That is clear. Thank you. One is grateful for one's message.

M: One is grateful for one's inquiry. Peace be upon one.

And upon one.

We will refer to the rays using the following as given to us by our guides:

Table 5 - The 12 Planetary Rays

RAY		Colour Range	Expressing Now as
1	Will and Power	Red	Divine Power, Will and Mission
2	Wisdom	Blue	Divine Wisdom
3	Active or Creative Intelligence	Yellow	Divine Light Technology and Science
4	Harmony	Green	Divine Peace and Harmony
5	Concrete Science	Orange	Divine Pattern Science at Group/Cosmic level
6	Abstract Idealism and Devotion	Indigo	Divine Ideal
7	Ceremonial Order	Violet	Divine Transmutation
8	Universal Cleansing	Blue Green	Universal Cleansing
9	Anchoring the Body of Light	Light Green/Lime	Divine Joy
10	Inviting the Soul Merge	Pearlescent	Oversoul and Monadic level consciousness
11	Bridging to Golden Earth	Orange Pink	The Triumvirate (Earth / Humanity / Source) Golden Earth
12	Anchoring Golden Earth and Christ Consciousness	Pure Level 3 Gold	Christ Consciousness, Soul and Monadic Consciousness

Ray 1: Divine Power, Will and Mission

This ray is of colour range red and is now expressed as divine power, will and mission. It is strongly focused on service to Golden Earth Mission currently.

Ray 2: Divine Wisdom

This ray is colour range blue and is now expressed as divine wisdom. It supports the stability and endurance of all work in service to Source, provides spiritual discernment and transpires divine.

Ray 3: Divine Light Technology and Science

This ray is colour range yellow and now corresponds to light technology and science. It infuses all scientific endeavours with divine guidance and the clarity of Source.

Ray 4: Divine Peace and Harmony

This ray is of colour emerald green and is now expressed as divine peace and harmony. It supports the resolution of all conflicts within one. It also supports empaths in the transformation of the empathy distortion to integrate divine compassion.

Ray 5: Divine Pattern Science at Group/Cosmic Level

This ray is of colour range orange and is now expressed as divine pattern science at group/cosmic level. It is through this ray that constellation information is coming to us.

Ray 6: Divine Ideal

This ray is of colour range indigo and is now expressed as divine ideal and devotion.

Ray 7: Divine Transmutation

This ray is of colour range violet and corresponds to divine transmutation of all which is not divine ideal or in divine will, which no longer serves and needs evolution.

Ray 8: Universal Cleansing

This ray is of colour range blue-green and has a cleansing energy that washes away the old which is not aligned with divine will. It operates at a universal level which includes planetary and cosmic.

Ray 9: Divine Joy

This ray is of colour range light green/lime and is now expressed as divine joy. It radiates unbounded joy across all levels, all bodies for all.

Ray 10: Oversoul and Monadic Level Consciousness

This ray is of pearlescent colour and is now expressed as oversoul and monadic level consciousness.

Ray 11: The Triumvirate (Earth / Humanity / Source) Golden Earth

This ray is of pink-orange colour range and is expressing The Triumvirate of Earth - Humanity - Source, Golden Earth.

Ray 12: Christ Consciousness, Soul and Monadic Consciousness

This ray is of gold colour and is expressing now as Christ consciousness, soul and monadic consciousness. It has the energy of Christ consciousness, all permeating love radiating all around and has also been called the ray of Christ consciousness. This ray is instantly manifesting and fulfilling the Divine's will, instantly transmuting what is in the way. It is also the highest integrated state of the threefold flame of love, wisdom and power.

How can you Work With Rays as a Parent?

We have mentioned that we are all the rays, however, it is useful for navigation purposes to know that there is a main constitutional ray for the personality (actually four, one for each body), for the oversoul and for the monad.

As this book is focusing on the path of the personality towards oversoul merge, we invite you as an adult to focus on your oversoul ray. Your oversoul ray is holding the main learnings, challenges and points of realisation that you will need to work on your soul merge path.

All rays can be called upon intentionally to infuse their energy into your body system and into a situation. They can support your clearing work at the personality level and enhance your everyday life. They are also, of course, very useful in your conscious connection to your oversoul and the embodiment of divine qualities, especially the main ray you are tasked to integrate for soul merge. Rays are here to support your spiritual growth and integration.

Balancing and developing the rays in your body system is a wonderful booster to your parenting path. We highly recommend that you dedicate part of your subtle senses development practice to tuning into the rays and feeling / sensing / hearing their energies. For example, you can talk to the rays and ask them how you can develop your connection to them, or you can ask your team in Spirit which ray would best serve you in a given situation. It is like a prayer directed to the rays. We also recommend that you read the related sections in Joshua David Stone's books: *The Complete Ascension Manual* and *Soul Psychology.*

You will also find specific exercises in the *Sourceness Journal* to work with the rays and receive support on your parenting path.

Identifying Your Oversoul Ray Type as a Parent

The following exploration helps you identify your oversoul ray. It is also possible to request confirmation and guidance from someone who is qualified to channel ray types. However, we encourage you to practise developing your own subtle sensing skills.

Exploration to Identify One's Oversoul Ray

Time: 15 mins. Recording available on www.sourceness.one website.

Begin by taking a few conscious, clearing and centring breaths and rest in your radiance. Say the oversoul mantra aloud or silently to yourself three times:
- I am the oversoul.
- I am the light divine.

- I am love divine.
- I am will divine.
- I am wisdom divine.
- I am power divine.
- I am divine design.

Then focusing and breathing in and out of your thymus– higher heart - enter your thymus chamber and sit on your throne of divinity and sovereignty in the middle of your thymus chamber. Allow the shift in consciousness. State your intention:

I am is in intendingness to identify the oversoul ray of (state your name).

Then visualise in front of you the picture below – diagram 17 - which looks like a compass.

One axis is showing the North-South, straight up and down. Another shows a diagonal line going from the Northwest to Southeast. Then another going from Northeast to Southwest. Just like a classic compass.

In the middle of this compass is a blue triangle. Go stand there facing North– that is facing the point or top of the triangle. This is your starting point. You may sense that it is a pyramid rather than a triangle… that's okay.

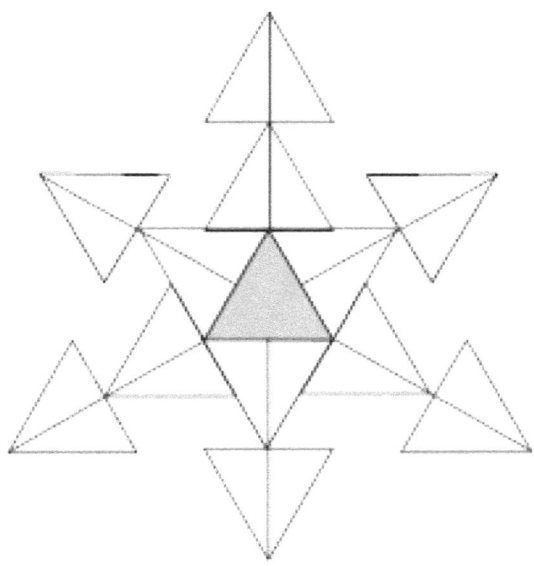

Diagram 17. The Ray Determination Compass

Sourceness: A Series for Golden Earth Being

Allow for guidance to come to you and see / sense / feel / know/ hear which direction you are guided to move towards and then turn towards that direction. In each direction, there are two triangles which will be in front of you.

Take a step in the first triangle. When you are standing on that triangle, ask for confirmation: "is this the triangle you are guiding me to stand on?" If it is, then stay there. If it's not, then move to the next triangle ahead of you. Ask again for confirmation. If it is then you are complete. If it's not, then return to the centre of the compass and repeat this process.

You can repeat this process as many times as you wish. We recommend that you do it three times in a row and get three times the confirmation of your matching triangle. Once you are done, return to the central triangle/pyramid and ask for the structure to be cleared as is ideal in alignment with divine will.

Then sitting in your throne of divinity and sovereignty in your thymus room, call on Lord Metatron to clear your thymus room with a pure light refresh. This will remove any impurity in the entire light structure that you are. When you feel complete, leave the thymus chamber.

You can find the corresponding ray number of the triangle you identified - in the first part of the exercise - in the diagram 16 (oversoul/monadic Ray determination compass with Ray numbers).

Write down your oversoul ray number for reference.

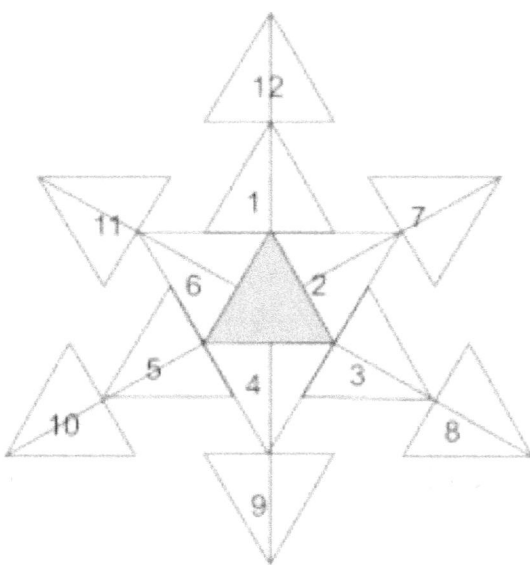

Diagram 18. Oversoul / Monadic Ray Determination Compass: with Ray Numbers

Parenting – Book One

How Can you Work with the Rays with Your Child?

With children, working with rays helps maintain the existing connection to the divine child and strengthen the bond with the oversoul. It will accelerate their spiritual growth and integration in ways we adults of this time cannot even yet imagine.

Discovering Your Child Through the Lens of the Rays

Becoming aware of the rays and learning to experiment with them is helpful to you and to your child. You can guide them in feeling and connecting to them in a playful way when they show interest. It is helpful to make a conscious link between the activities your child is interested in or activities you can offer and your child's monadic ray type.

If your child shows interests for activities which you don't necessarily relate to nor understand, it is encouraged to give them the space to explore, requesting ideal protection and support for them to their oversoul and team in Spirit. As parents we may not understand how important these activities are for the child's soul. As we learn about their monadic ray, we can become more attuned to their exploration.

A child with a strong monadic connection to:

- Ray 1 will be inclined to explore divine destruction, leadership and willpower
- Ray 2 will be interested in the wisdom of God and ask questions to grow one's understanding. This child will enjoy spending time in Nature and observe the change in luminosity, sunsets and sunrises…
- Ray 3 will be inclined to activities which involve mental capabilities - engineering and crafts, robotics, experimentations and discoveries, building and envisioning, architecture…
- Ray 4 will be inclined to all sorts of arts, beauty as well as opposition and conflict. You may find the child in exploration of Ray 4 quite temperamental and conflictual.
- Ray 5 will be inclined to research, investigation, scientific experimentation, understanding the structures behind objects and phenomena and will have a great sense of observation.
- Ray 6 will be inclined to do things in a way that signifies and expresses devotion and love. What they do is not as important as how they do it and they need the time and space and tools to do it the way that best pleases the divine in them.
- Ray 7 will be inclined to order and the exploration of magic, the occult and the mysteries of life. They will enjoy fantastic stories and fantasy worlds, spending hours in their creative inner world in contact with other worlds and the invisible to the adult eye. Children exploring this ray need protection against dark and manipulative forces.

- Ray 8 will be inclined to healing and balancing what is out of balance. They may show an interest to visit places that are out of balance, or on the contrary, require regeneration in highly energised oases. It is important to listen to the needs of a child with a strong ray 8 connection when they request quiet and rest.
- Ray 9, will be inclined to joy and experiences that strengthen, amplify and communicate joy. Children with a strong connection to Ray 9 thrive in joyful settings and reunions, enjoy playfulness, celebrations and joy attuned music. They are content with very little in nature and need a lot of freedom to do their work.
- Ray 10 will be inclined to communicating with the angelic realm and pure beings such as unicorns. They will enjoy graceful activities such as dancing to classical or gentle music or angel painting, harp music and any activity which involves silence and contemplation.
- Ray 11 will be inclined to serve Earth and bring about the Golden Age. They thrive in collective work outdoors or related to the land, to touching elements and maybe cooking together.
- Ray 12 will be inclined to go in depth in what sparks their interest and reveal the all-encompassing connection and love of wholeness in the specific activity or interest.

Your child has certainly a strong monadic connection with more than one ray and some combinations can be quite surprising. For example, the combination of the fiery Ray 1 and the angelic Ray 10. It is useful to be aware as parents of which rays your child is naturally embodying and observe which ones they begin to grow and integrate. This can be of tremendous help to support them in the offering of activities you make to them, places you take them, the protected freedom you give to them, and the speed, space and silence you create around them.

The Professional Path of Your Child

How can you Work with Rays as a Parent?

In his excellent summary about the Rays, Joshua David Stone suggested links between the ray types and the chosen professions: for example, a Ray 1 person is inclined to leadership roles, a Ray 3 person chooses a profession in engineering and science. As mentioned, we highly recommend you read the Joshua David Stone material.

While there is a link between ray and professional occupation, the link has become more complex in recent years. Especially as we are advancing on the mission Golden Earth, there are, for example, many Ray 1 types who are called to do the work of divine destruction and bring their leadership throughout various professions in society that need an upgrade at the very core and not necessarily in the top leadership positions where more Ray 2 types are called to be in service to open up divine wisdom at the top of societal structures. One can employ the rays in different settings and for various missions. As a parent, keeping an open mind and tuning to observe the truth of your child in this divine now moment can be helpful in guiding their professional choices.

Studies and professional paths are oftentimes a source of great concern for parents. We invite you to make a list of your beliefs about schooling, education, professional occupation and what is important to the well-being of your child's soul and personality.

We are guided to share the following about Golden Earth which came through our guide and teacher Telonis:

- In Golden Earth, status is an irrelevant societal consideration: all work and action being soul driven and all souls being in service to Source, Earth and Humanity, there is no self-aggrandisement, self-deflation or comparison between souls - these are all personality drivers. Ambition and achievements are also irrelevant for these are also personality drivers.
- In Golden Earth, there are no heroes, no victims, no perpetrators. There is no cause to fight for - all activism stems from limitedness. Soul merge implies that all soul extensions have an inherent understanding that their life is in service to others.
- In Golden Earth, financial considerations will become irrelevant because money will no longer be used as a power currency. All that is needed in service to Source, Earth and humanity will be provided.

The focus of work is not to earn a living but to fulfil the soul missions and tasks one is called to work on.

Please reflect on the above and listen carefully to the voices of your personality and the voice of your soul. What are you guided to hold as your intention for Golden Earth and for your child's soul?

What are Soul Merge Challenges for Each of the 12 Rays?

While it is intended for all to integrate all rays, at each level there is a predominant ray which is constitutional, and which is the one to be integrated for that level. It is more complex than this and we do not only work with one ray at each stage. However, to focus our conscious awareness on what is essential, we are guided to simplify the process by consciously working with one ray at a time.

The following table channelled through Mahatma for this book provides a summary of the main topics and learnings your child is likely to work with on their path towards monadic merge for each of the monadic ray types. This table is also useful for you as a parent because the challenges and learnings are similar. However, this table is specifically channelled for the monadic merge which is the next stage after soul merge. As you have read already, many children are already soul merged and even if their soul merge may not be complete, we are guided to recommend that the focus be placed on working with their monadic ray. The monadic ray is an accelerator of soul sovereignty. As you help your child consciously work with and integrate their monadic ray, this will help them tremendously on their spiritual path and will also accelerate the divine plan for Golden Earth.

Table 6 - Main Topics and Learnings on the Path for each Monadic Ray

Ray 1	Divine Power, Will and Mission	Leadership, boundaries, personal power, personal vs. collective will, assertiveness, anger, rejection, hatred, service, humility, acceptance
Ray 2	Divine Wisdom	Personality and spiritual discernment, love of knowledge, learning, equanimity, divine order, observation, non-judgement, divine clarity, stewardship of Earth
Ray 3	Divine Light Technology and Science	Learning to work with light technologies in scientific pursuit, overcoming right and wrong, exploring truth, exploring light structures beyond the visible, superficiality and depth, service, scientific exhilaration and humility
Ray 4	Divine Peace and Harmony	Conflict, wars, resolution, peace, harmony, divine equilibrium, justice (overcoming the illusion of injustice), forgiveness, divine compassion
Ray 5	Divine Pattern Science at Group/Cosmic level	Stepping beyond consensus reality, connecting invisible dots, encompassing greater connection to other life forms (incl. extra-terrestrial, elemental...), navigation agility between soul levels, mathematics, quantum physics, exploration of the unknown
Ray 6	Divine Ideal	Service to others and Source, overcoming servitude, bigotry and dogmatism, overcoming idealism, romanticism and sentimentalism, overcoming all love distortions, self-love, transforming modesty into humility and compassion, spiritual growth
Ray 7	Divine Transmutation	Insight vs. imagination, resolution of bonds, contracts, agreements... with lower astral planes and religious groups, overcoming interference with lower astral planes, mastery in divine clearing and transmutation tools, self-healer, divine responsibility, channelling, religious order
Ray 8	Universal Cleansing	Divine trinity of Source - Humanity and Earth, divine purity, trinity healing, regeneration, universal level cleansing, restoring divine will, facing misalignment with divine will
Ray 9	Divine Joy	Unbounded joy, freedom, highlighting limitations, divine/spiritual indifference

Ray 10	Oversoul and Monadic level consciousness	Conscious constellations (family, corporate/organisational and nations)
Ray 11	The Triumvirate (Earth / Humanity / Source) Golden Earth	Golden Earth radiance, divine balance, divine perfection, unlimitedness
Ray 12	Christ Consciousness, Oversoul and Monadic Consciousness	Christ consciousness integration at oversoul and monad levels

How to Identify Your Child's Monadic Ray?

The process to identify your child's monadic ray is the same as described above to find the parent's oversoul ray (and you may of course when you feel guided to use the same process to identify your monadic ray). There is no restriction in knowing already what your monadic ray is. However, this may change as you complete the soul merge. Interestingly, unlike astrological birth charts which are fixed and determined by one's birthplace and time, one's constitutional rays can evolve. For this reason, it is important to state a clear intention when you do these explorations: soul merge or monadic merge. This is also not restricted: you may use the same exploration and ask guidance about which ray can best support you in this time or for a particular task or occasion. The response you get is determined by your intention.

PART FIVE: DELIMITEDNESS

The fruit of parenting as a light path and living from your sourceness is to become a delimited adult. What we mean by this is that you access your full power God-self potential within the fixed design of your divine blueprint for this incarnation. A delimited person is all loving, anchored in their divine wisdom and limitless in their power in service to their oversoul/monad and Source. This is what Golden Earth is about: humans radiate pure golden light because they have transmuted all the limitations weighing on them and they dedicate their lifeforce to their soul's missions and tasks working together in harmonious group consciousness.

The path to delimited-ness is one of self-healing one's limitations to fully radiate one's true being. This book is a bridge to Golden Earth and this part is about supporting your path towards it.

Chapter 1
The Language of Parenting

The reality you experience directly stems from the conclusions of your personality and the repeated/magnetised thoughts and emotions which your bodies focus on. Words expressed out loud or in your mind become your reality, especially if they carry emotion. The stronger the emotion or the more recurrent the thought, even more so the combination of both, the more solid the experience seems.

Language Delimitation

Conscious parenting invites you to look at and choose the thoughts you allow in your mind and the words you express. The spoken word through the intent and the emotion it carries sends out the vibration of what you are asking to experience. There is nothing which you experience which is not crafted within you. The words you usually or recurrently speak carry the energetics of your personality's conclusions and are linked to programs within you. They make an interesting clue to what these programs are about and invite you to investigate whether they are still serving you or not.

For example, we invite you to explore and reconsider words which carry limitations:
- Never/always
- Impossible
- Can't / not able / incapable
- Should / shouldn't / must / mustn't / have to…
- All judgements towards yourself and others disguised as feelings (for example: worried, stressed, rejected, criticised, punished, abandoned, abused…)
- All unloving words towards yourself/child and others - by unloving we mean words which carry fear or are not unconditionally loving
- Thought forms which keep you stuck in the collective unconscious (for example: the grass is greener on the other side)

The language we use can give us fascinating insight on our unconscious inner programming. You begin by becoming aware of your language and the words/expressions you use which are limiting you; then find the underlying programming and clear it. This is the most effective way to reprogram your language: when you carry unconditional love programs instead of fear programs within you, your language naturally changes too.

Intentional Sound Vibration

The difference between the thought and the spoken word is the expressed sound of the vibration. When you practise conscious language and speaking, the attention is not only on the word, but also the sound of it, the intention behind it and the energy contained in it. This links to the chosen intention that moves the words through you. The language of conscious parenting involves a conscious choice of intention. For example, the intention and tonality you put behind calling your child's name makes a great difference in the message you send to them. When you work towards infusing everything you say with the intention of unconditional love, not only your language changes, but also the tonality of your voice.

Your Language and the Energy of the Rays

One of the experiments we encourage you to do is to intentionally request a specific ray you call upon to embrace your words with its energy and notice the difference. For example, if you seek authority and leadership, request your words to be embraced by Ray 1; if you seek to bring resolution between your children having a fight, ask your words to be embraced by Ray 4; if you would like to bring calm and relaxation in an (overly) active household call on Ray 2...

There are countless possibilities for you to explore. For example, you can ask that your mental body be embraced in a specific ray and therefore your thoughts will be infused with the energy of this ray and the mental vibration you emit will be aligned with this ray. We encourage you experiment playfully - always request guidance and ensure that your experiments are aligned with divine will and are for the benefit of all.

Calling Forth Your Child's Ideal State

We have mentioned various times in this book that what we put our attention on grows. In your daily interactions with your child, it can be a challenge not to be caught in the personality grabs and find oneself interacting personality to personality. It is also necessary for your child to experiment and explore their personality and operate from the personality level and therefore be caught in drama and the experience of limiting conclusions and programs.

As a parent, you may not know what the ideal resolution in each situation is or what your child (oversoul) is exactly intending to experience and learn in a given context. It may also not be straightforward to identify if a challenge is the expression of a limiting programming or a genuine soul challenge on the path of your child.

The urge to comfort our child, protect her, advise him to avoid mistakes and painful experiences is a personality drive which requires your scrutiny. There is an ideal way to be with your child in situations of challenge which both acknowledges her and remains 100% spiritually indifferent to their experience and compassionate with their soul. You do not need to know whether the situation is due to a program or part of their soul journey: you can instead pray for them to receive the ideal help they need and bring forth with your intention their ideal healed state.

What do we mean by ideal healed state? This is the state of completed growth and integration of the oversoul for this specific learning. You do not need to know what the learning is specifically, nor what the state is; you can still call it forth through intention by attuning to unconditional love. This requires your divine trust in your child's path and in their ability to find within themselves the resources they need. As you hold this intention, you are opening the possibility in the field of potentials and helping them access it. The clearer and purer your field, the clearer it will be for them to discern what is needed. Oftentimes, no words are needed - simple statements thought with unconditional love or whispered to their heart will suffice:

"I fully trust you will find the way"

"I love you and I know you have all you need to navigate this".

Chapter 2
Self-Healing

As we were preparing this book and while we were being guided to examine inputs from existing sources, the clear message came through to become our own Light and healer. For some this is already a driving force, while for others it may be a growth stage.

What our guidance tells us, is that at this stage of humanity, it is willed by the Divine that every parent (being) reclaims their soul sovereignty, builds a direct connection to their sourceness and accesses within all the support they need to be healthy and thriving adults. What the Divine also wills is that these adults parent in alignment with divine will and for the highest well-being of their children's oversouls, provide guidance and healing to the children under their responsibility.

This process involves the acceptance of oneself as one's own healer.

The conventional approach to health is fragmented: the medical system is based on specialisation, looking at the parts without integrating the whole. Although there is an increasing movement of medical practitioners who are intuitively and through their own experiential path integrating a more holistic approach and working in close collaboration with healing practitioners to bring the pieces of the puzzle together, this is still not the norm, and it will take a while until it is fully at the desired level that the Divine wills.

What we are inviting you to consider is that the keys to your health at all levels are within you. In the new era, there will of course be healers, but everyone will be responsible for and in control of their health. Much of what we consider today to be in the domain of experts will be available to individuals, for example, the healing of:
- Physical pains
- Mental disorders
- Fears and phobias
- Emotional disorders
- Ancestral related ailments
- Past life related ailments
- The origin of chronic ailments

What is an Ailment?

We are all unique in energetic make-up, meaning each energetic system contains a unique package of 'electrons' (we use the term for simplicity although it is not exactly accurate). Each of the 'electrons' in each system is uniquely charged. This means that a one-size-fits-all approach will not work for humans... A shift is required to embrace the unique complexity that we are, and at the same time to resist the temptation to be evangelical about any solution - it may work for your system, but this doesn't mean it will work for anyone else.

Ailments/disease do not originate only in the physical body: there is always an energetic root to disease which connects to our other bodies and eventually it will manifest in the densest energy body which is the physical body.

Essential Principles - Guiding Principles

The approach we offer in this book, is based on the following guiding principles:
- The purpose of healing is to experience unconditional love, divine power and higher wisdom which we already are, in all our bodies. When we are aligned with our sourceness within, we are healthy.
- At the soul level, we have agreed to any ailment we experience in our incarnation. It may also be part of a spiritual journey to choose to experience physical illness.
- An ailment is an abnormal condition in one or more bodies. By abnormal we mean out of balance for the normal health of that person. All ailments are of energetic nature and depending on which body they are affecting; they have a more or less dense vibration. Ailments can be caused by living beings (e.g., bacteria, virus, entities) or energetic structures (e.g., program, cord, loyalty, spells…).
- Life on Earth, as we experience it, is holographic. This means that images / imprints / threads… which we can call experiences for simplification, are simultaneously projected and experienced on various dimensions differently. Total healing implies healing in all dimensions, levels, realities, bodies, times and space/lifetimes.
- Some ailments you experience in this incarnation are not aligned with your oversoul path and may beresidues and programs from other lives - they require clearing / transmuting / healing.
- Healing follows the intention to heal. In many cases, the healing intention is even enough to clear an ailment.
- All is willed by the Divine and healing is always available to us upon request as aligned with divine will and timing.
- There is no benefit to continue to experience suffering and no longer any need to experience it, in the sense that once aware of 'one is suffering' one can choose a different experience. Suffering exists energetically within human grids as numerous programs - these programs may have been concluded in other lives, may have been acquired unconsciously, maybe passed within ancestral grids. Going back to what we shared about the conclusions our oversoul may have reached in other lives, a conclusion such as 'suffering is part of the human experience' may be residing in the 'bucket of our personality.' Please see page 187 on how to remove common programs from your bucket!

- Whatever you give your focused attention to, grows; what you give energy to, you become. Total healing is an expression of unified integrated energy.
- Ultimate healing is the experience of sourceness, surrenderedness to sourceness and total acceptance of divine will.

Basic Energetic Clearing for Parents

The following is a thorough basic energetic clearing we are guided to take you through.

The purpose of this basic clearing is to: remove extraneous programming that is non-serving; remove entities that are non-serving; clear channels within your energy system so that communication/energy can flow between your personality and soul and monad; clear any toxic inflows that are coming into your energy system which you will not be conscious of but which may be affecting how you are; and, clear the essential structure of your energy system so that pure energy can be received and absorbed.

After doing this clearing you may feel tired, sleepy, achy, like you have flu. There will be a period of integration which may last for a day or a week. Self-care is essential during integration so sleep as you need to, drink pure water and no alcohol, eat lightly. It is therefore important to time the completion of this clearing when you have a convenient window that is not loaded with work, etc.

Please prepare before doing this exercise. Read it through at least once. Set time aside to do this exercise (it will take about 10 minutes) followed by a few minutes of quiet time in silence for yourself. It is best if you can be alone when doing this, but it's not essential. You do not want to be disturbed or interrupted while doing it, if possible.

Essential Basic Clearing –
Personality Level 16.01.2024

Channelled from Metatron by personality Lorna Collins.

Why is this needed?
Metatron speaks,
Greetings dear ones. We are grateful to you that you choose to receive our message today. This message brings clarity to your essential nature. Your personality level, also known as the soul extension level, is the foundation level of your energetic system operation here on Earth. To progress and grow to this level, it must be cleared of blocks and obstacles. Many of you have spent much time and energy on this task and yet still find blocks.
We, the spiritual hierarchy, have decided at this time to release this essential clearing to all so that it may be used to accelerate your spiritual growth process.
It is not necessary to understand all the language or information in this clearing.

Your intention is all that is necessary.

Your intention is 'I am (oversoul) commits to receive support to clear what may be cleared in this divine moment so that the oversoul blueprint, the reason and mission for my personality here on Earth, may be realised.'

With this commitment the clearing of your energy system (five bodies, physical, etheric, emotional, mental and spiritual, subconscious and conscious mind and your central channel connections) will be aligned as is ideal for you. All will be aligned with divine will and with your oversoul blueprint.

We are ever with you. Loving and supporting you. Call us for help.

In service.

Metatron

When you are ready, begin with saying aloud three times the Soul Mantra and go to your thymus chamber.

    Soul Mantra:
    I am the soul
    I am the light divine
    I am love divine
    I am will divine
    I am wisdom divine
    I am power divine
    I am divine design.

Take your awareness to your thymus chamber. Then, please read slowly aloud and with intent the following text and allow it to sink in, pausing in between each line. There is also a recording available for this.

- "I AM calls upon Lord Metatron, Lord of Light, Mahatma, Avatar of Synthesis and Melchizedek, the Universal Logos, my team in Spirit of the purest light and resonance, my oversoul and monad to come be with me now and work in harmonious group consciousness in alignment with divine ideal and divine will to conduct this basic clearing of (says your full name) personality level, human energy system, five bodies, physical, etheric, emotional, mental and spiritual, and the subconscious mind and higher mind and of central channel.
- I am activates the alignment of the divine consciousness of (say your full name) reconnecting to my I AM presence,
- Reconnecting me to my I AM presence,
- I am asks for activation of the Monadic Rescue,
- I am asks to be located and united to the monad and oversoul in all bodies, linked in all dimensions and timelines manifested in the Universal grid,
- I am asks for activation of the connection to one's team in Spirit of the purest light and resonance, all helpers, guides, guardians and other angels, teachers and star-beings,
- I am asks for my Primal Soul to help and manifest in wisdom, guidance, healing, protection, clarity.
- I am asks for one's three-fold flame to be manifest and activated , no exceptions.

- I am asks that unconditional love, divine wisdom of spiritual consciousness, divine will, be anchored in the three-fold flame of (state your name), expand through the grid.
- I am asks Source to clear all blocks to zero time, clear all blocks to working alpha to omega to all levels and depths of creation.
- I am asks Source to clear one's soul and energy system of all programming, including separate downloaded programming, entities, extra beings, multiple beings, separate beings, extra souls, multiple souls of all categories back a 1000 generations.
- I am asks for all energies in all levels, bodies, dimensions, no exceptions, that are non-serving of the one to be cleared, as is divine ideal and as is in divine will.
- I am asks Source to clear all entities that are non-serving of the one, in all levels, bodies, dimensions, no exceptions, as is divine ideal and as is in divine will.
- I am asks Source to clear the personality (soul extension - lower self) and soul of (state your name) of highly blocking, tricking, intriguing or sabotaging programmes, re-generation programmes, time sensitive programs attached, hidden, disguised, or shielded, no exceptions in all levels, bodies, dimensions, no exceptions, as is divine ideal and as is in divine will.
- I am asks Source to clear all energy that no longer serves (say your full name) from one's energy system, as is divine ideal and as is in divine will.
- I am asks Source to clear, seal, repair for (say your name) all portals and openings to lower dimensions, as is divine ideal and as is in divine will.
- I am asks Source to seal all etheric tears or openings in the etheric body of (say your full name) that no longer serve the one, as is divine ideal and in alignment with divine will.
- I am seals, seals, seals my Pillar of Light.
- I am asks for triple shields of Ultraviolet Light, to the power of three times three, to be placed in one's Pillar of Light.
- I am clears to infinity, clears to infinity, clears to infinity, one's entire energy system, all bodies, all levels, all universes, no exceptions, as is divine ideal and as is in divine will.
- I am asks Source to place an Ultraviolet Ray shield around one's Earth Star chakra to prevent replays and reactivations of ancestral programming, as is divine ideal and as is in divine will.
- I am asks Source to clear one's Earth Star chakra to infinity, clear to infinity, clear to infinity.
- I am asks Source to place an Ultraviolet Ray shield around one's Soul Star chakra to prevent replays and reactivations of soul family programming.
- I am asks Source to clear my Soul Star to infinity, clear to infinity, clear to infinity.
- I am asks Source to clear all conscious and subconscious clutter in one's energy system, clear to infinity, clear to infinity.
- I am asks Source to clear all world energies in my energy system, clear to infinity, clear to infinity.

- I am asks Source to update, upgrade, elevate, educate all committees, all-star beings, align me to the highest level of all committees, souls, monads, guides, star councils, star beings, committees to the highest level of light, radiant love to Golden Earth.
- I am asks Source to clear all channels to the oversoul and monad of (say your full name).
- I am asks Source to ensure oversoul and monads are working together for divine ideal, highest well-being of all, as is divine ideal and as is in alignment with divine will.
- I am asks Source to ensure that all teams in Spirit are working together in the highest harmonious group consciousness for the highest well-being of all, as is divine ideal for all, in alignment with divine will. All teams are working together. Bring Medical Corp online.
- I am calls on the oversoul and monad of (say your name) to please research and find all portals, then clear, close, seal with clearest, purest light, all portals and all openings, in all times, dimensions, spaces, realities and levels, no exceptions which do not serve (say your name). Close and lock all openings and return the keys to Source, disappear all now.
- I am calls on the oversoul and monad of (say your full name) to please find all disguised and hidden, magically or otherwise, portals, doors, access points, tunnels, pipes that no longer serve, and seal them all with light and neutralise them so that none are harmful to me or any other being.
- I am asks Source to identify all time sensitive or time activated programmes that do not serve me and remove all programs now, all levels, all dimensions, no exceptions and asks Source to remove all regeneration programs attached to these, from all levels, no exceptions, as is divine ideal and as is in divine will.
- I am asks Source to seal and close all openings to back accesses on the Earth plane, please lock all openings and return the keys to Source. Disappear now.
- I am asks Source to remove all programming associated with these portals at all levels, dimensions, realities, universes and stations, lifetimes, time space, no exceptions, as is divine ideal and as is in divine will.
- I am asks Source to remove any regeneration programs attached, all levels, no exceptions, as is divine ideal and as is in divine will.

For (say your name) please remove completely all energy cords in my system which do not serve me, transmute, with love and light as appropriate. Seal, seal, seal.

- I am asks Source to fill my system with purest light as is ideal for me.
- I am asks Source to seal the energy system of (say your full name) and fill all toxic streams that are contributing to any portal with pure love and light. Neutralise all toxic streams so that none of them are harmful to me (say your name) or to any other being.
- I am seals one's energy system with love, light, spirit, life.
- I am asks that all connections to the 12 mighty divine light grids be adjusted as is ideal for me in alignment with divine will, and please harmonise, balance and restore to divine equilibrium as is ideal for one.

- I am asks Source to close all multidimensional openings, tunnels, vortexes, channels, bleed-throughs, that do not serve me (say your name) for this incarnation as is divine ideal and divine will.
- I am asks Source to remove all etheric woundings, tears, openings and anything else that needs repairing, but which the one has not mentioned, but which the ONE knows needs to be removed, in the etheric body/level and in any level or body, in all dimensions, no exceptions, as is divine ideal and as is in divine will.
- I am asks Source to remove all etheric and psychic debris in all bodies, all levels, all dimensions, no exceptions, as is divine ideal and as is in divine will.
- I am asks Source to open one's pathway between subconscious mind, conscious mind and higher mind, and superconscious mind.
- I am asks Source to repair and restore all auric levels – all levels, no exceptions and restore to divine ideal as is divine will.
- I am asks Source to activate permanent atoms as is divine ideal and in divine will.
- I am asks Source to activate ideal grounding and anchoring to ensure that the soul extension (your name) is nurtured and energised as is divine ideal and in alignment with divine will.
- One wills it so.
- Peace and gratitude be upon you.

Basic Energetic Clearing for Children

Once you have done the basic energetic clearing for yourself and feel ready to do it for your child, then follow this guidance. Please do this work on one child at a time. Realise that they will also need integration time, so best not to do it if they are going to school the next day or if they have heavy commitments. Holidays may be the best time. For parents to do on behalf of their child. Please prepare before doing this exercise. Read it through at least once. Set time aside to do this exercise (it will take about 10 minutes) and follow by a few minutes of quiet time in silence for yourself. You can be alone when doing this. You may wish to do this with your child but it's not essential. You do not want to be disturbed or interrupted while doing it, if possible.

When you are ready, begin with saying out loud three times the soul mantra and centre yourself, go to your Thymus chamber. Then, please read slowly aloud and with intent the following text and allow it to sink in, pausing in between each line.

I AM,
I activate the alignment of the divine consciousness of (say your full name) reconnecting to my I AM presence, Reconnecting me to my I AM presence; I call on my team in Spirit of the purest light and resonance to come be with me now. I call on my soul and monad, and the soul and monad and team of my child (say their full name) to work in harmonious group consciousness with us all.
I ask to activate the Monadic Rescue for (say child's full name).
I ask for (say child's full name) to be located or united to the Monad and Oversoul in all bodies,

linked in all dimensions and timelines, manifested, pulse in the Universal grid.
I ask for (say child's full name) to be connected to one's team in Spirit of the purest light and resonance, all helpers, guides, guardian and other angels, teachers and star-beings, be activated,
I ask for (say child's full name) Oversoul to help and manifest in wisdom, guidance, healing, protection, clarity.
I ask for (say child's full name) three-fold flame in all bodies and dimensions to be activated and manifested, no exceptions.
Please anchor unconditional love, divine wisdom of spiritual consciousness, divine will, in the three-fold flame of (say child's full name) expand through the grid.
Dear Spirit please clear for (say child's full name) all blocks to zero time,
Please clear all blocks to working alpha to omega to all levels and depths of creation.
Please clear (say child's full name) soul and monad and energy system of all programming, including separate downloaded programming, entities, extra beings, multiple beings, separate beings, extra souls, multiple souls of all categories back to a 1000 generations.
Please clear all non-serving entities in (say child's full name) energy system in all levels, bodies, dimensions, no exceptions.
Please clear the personality of (say child's full name) (soul extension - lower self) and soul of (say child's full name) of highly blocking, tricking, intriguing or sabotaging programmes, re-generation programmes, time sensitive programs attached, hidden, disguised or shielded, no exceptions in all levels, bodies, dimensions, no exceptions.
Please clear all that no longer serves (say child's full name) energy system.
Please clear for (say child's full name) all portals and openings to lower dimensions that are non-serving, lock and return key to source.
Please seal any etheric tears or openings in the etheric body of (say child's full name).
Please place triple shields of ultraviolet flame around the entire energy system of (say child's full name) to the power of 3 times 3 with light. Please seal the Pillar of Light of (say child's full name).
Please clear the entire energy system of (say child's full name), all bodies, all levels, all universes, no exceptions, to infinity, clear to infinity, clear to infinity.
Please place an ultraviolet fire shield around the Earth Star chakra of (say child's full name) to prevent replays and reactivation of ancestral programming.
Please clear the Earth Star chakra of (say child's full name) to infinity, clear to infinity, clear to infinity.
Please place an ultraviolet flame shield around the Soul Star chakra of (say child's full name) to prevent replays and activations of soul family programming.
Please clear the Soul Star of (say child's full name) to infinity, clear to infinity, clear to infinity.
Please clear all conscious and subconscious clutter for (say child's full name).
Please clear all world energies for (say child's full name).
Please update, upgrade, elevate, educate all (say child's full name) councils and committees, all-star beings, align my child to the highest level of all councils and committees, souls, monads, guides, star councils,

*star beings, committees to the highest level of light, radiant love to the new paradigm.
Please clear all channels of (say child's full name) to their soul and monad.*

Please ensure the soul and monads of (say child's full name) are working together. Ensure that all Teams in Spirit are working together in purest harmonious group consciousness for the ideal wellbeing of all in alignment with divine will. All teams are working together. Bring Medical Corp online.

I call on the soul and monad of (say child's full name) to please research and find all portals, clear, close, seal with clearest, purest light, all portals and all openings, in all times, dimensions, spaces, realities and levels, no exceptions which do not serve. Close, and lock all and return the keys to Source, disappear now.

I call on the soul and monad of (say child's full name) to please find all disguised and hidden, magically or otherwise, portals, doors, access points, tunnels, pipes that no longer serve, and seal them with light and neutralise them so that none are harmful to me or any other being. Please identify all time sensitive or time activated programmes and remove now, all levels, all dimensions, no exceptions. Please also remove any regeneration programs attached to them.

For (say child's full name) please seal and close all back accesses on the Earth plane, and all openings to those accesses, lock and return the key to Source. Disappear now.

For (say child's full name) please remove all programming associated with these portals at all levels, dimensions, realities, universes and stations, lifetimes, time space, no exceptions. Please remove any regeneration programs attached, all levels, no exceptions.

For (say child's full name) please remove completely all non-serving energy cords, transmute, with love and light as appropriate. Seal afterwards. Fill the energy system of (say child's full name) with purest light as is ideal for them.

Please seal the energy system of (say child's full name) and fill all toxic streams that are contributing to any portal with pure love and light. Neutralise all toxic streams so that none of them are harmful to (say child's full name) or to any other being.

Please seal the energy system of (say child's full name) with love, light, spirit, life.

For (say child's full name) please close all multidimensional openings, tunnels, vortexes, channels, bleed-throughs, that are non-serving for this incarnation.

For (say child's full name) please remove all etheric woundings, tears, openings and anything else that needs repairing but which I have not mentioned, in the etheric body/level and in any level or body, in all dimensions, no exceptions.

For (say child's full name) please remove all etheric and psychic debris in all bodies, all levels, all dimensions, no exceptions.

For (say child's full name) please repair and restore all auric levels – all levels to restore to divine ideal as is in divine will.

For (say child's full name) please activate permanent atoms as is ideal for them. One wills it so. Peace and gratitude be upon you.

Recognizing and Working with Triggers

Once you have put in place a foundational level of protection and clearing in your body system, you can begin the work of clearing what is non-aligned within you.

Conscious parenting is about shifting your basis of operation from a focus on the personality level only to integrating the soul level. This involves the personal work of healing, transforming, transmuting, clearing... what in your personality is not serving you in this current incarnation. In our garden analogy, it is about clearing the weeds and brambles which are blocking the plants that you want to see grow in your garden.

A very effective way to spot your inner weeds and brambles is to work with triggers.

Understanding Triggers

Triggers are easier to identify than they are to explain, because they're based on our individual experiences: it is possible for anything to be a trigger. A trigger is a *person, place, thing, situation or experience that elicits an intense or unexpected emotional response.*

When you are triggered, this is a sign that something has been stirred within you and this is usually a program in your personality. This is very valuable information in your conscious parenting work because it gives you an indication of the type of belief and story that are registered as conclusions in you. There is no point to focus your attention on changing the outer condition that generates the trigger. Instead working with the trigger means to turn your attention inwards and find out what is there within you that got stimulated/activated and generates an automatic response.

Recognizing Triggers

Triggers are not "threats", but rather a non-threatening stimulus of our stress (fight-or-flight) response. Here are some ways to recognize when you might be triggered:
- Notice how you feel - Do you feel anxious, overwhelmed, or are you having trouble calming yourself down? Pay attention to these symptoms when they arise, particularly if they feel sudden or unrelated to your circumstances. If you're feeling this way but you don't know why, there's a good chance that you're triggered.
- Something is bothering you - Is there something that's suddenly weighing on your mind? If it's a major issue, your concern might not be out of the ordinary. But if it's a routine occurrence that's got you stressed, there might be more to it than meets the eye.
- Listen to yourself - We've all had times when we can't seem to stop venting about a particular issue. We think we've put it out of our minds, but when we talk about it, we feel worked up all over again. If you find that you can't stop rehashing a particular situation, something about it may have triggered you.

- Check your composure - Trigger reactions are notoriously explosive. After all, there's a reason why the term "hair trigger" became a popular metaphor. If you find that you're having an outsized reaction (or many of them), pay attention. You may not be reacting to the situation at hand, but to an underlying stressor.

Becoming Aware of Your Identification

Being your own healer or self-healing requires that you are aware of your own well-being at many levels: physical, emotional, mental/psychological and spiritual. This requires that you are able to see / sense / feel / know what is going on inside of you and these multiple levels, and involves a dedicated practice of self-awareness, self-observation/self-examination in a detached way as we described earlier so that you are able to realistically and objectively spot what is going on. The beginning point of self-healing is to be 100% self-loving which enables us to access the healing power of our oversoul. **We do not heal the personality from the personality level.**

One of the main areas of work is what you identify with: identification has an impact on all of your bodies, your energy system, your polarities and more.

All personality identity is a construct whether the construction is in service or dis-service to us, whether it is conscious or unconscious, whether it is our own making or inherited, whether it is built in this lifetime or has been in place already before this incarnation. As such, it can be transformed if need be. We do not have an inherent personality: as we mentioned earlier, the personality is a bucket.

As you progress on your path towards soul merge, you will find that personality is less and less of a need. The soul doesn't rely on personality to live and enjoy its experiences. Naturally, you will simply find yourself more pliant, adaptable and water-like when it comes to defining who you are. At some point, it will even seem irrelevant to you. The new era for Earth will not operate through the personality level and identity will gradually disappear.

All identification is a personality process, including identification with Source. When one says I AM THAT I AM, one is not identifying with I AM, one is in being-ness or being in the divine NOW moment. One is having an experience but one is not the experience, nor the experiencer. At the soul level, there are no identifications.

Identification implies thought - forms, patterns, programming... and these very often have an emotional aspect linked to them. Thoughts trigger emotions which in turn trigger our experience of reality. It is indeed that simple: all of your experience is created in your mind.

It is also useful to mention that identification at group level is more powerful and therefore more manipulative than individual identification: the larger the group, the stronger the energy behind the beliefs, thought forms, patterns... For example, if you live in a neighbourhood which strongly believes that children should have many extra-curricular activities and your child goes to the local school with children whose parents strongly believe in extra-curricular activity, even a slight belief within you that extra-curricular activity is supporting your child will by means of the group consciousness have a much greater impact on you than if you were living in a neighbourhood which didn't care about it at all without you even realising it. The moment you identify with the belief, the group consciousness is impacting you in a much stronger way than if the belief was individual. This is a very important point because seldom are your beliefs individual.

In conscious parenting, we invite you to be aware of your identifications and transcend them. A simple and effective way to spot if you are under the grip of identification is to ask yourself:

- Am I in a story?
- Am I telling myself a story here?
- What story am I experiencing here?

When you practise detached observation of your identifications you can consciously work with them and shift your conclusions.

We highly recommend that you set your intention on clearing all identification for one simple reason: you don't need it. As mentioned, identification is an attachment.

My Intention is to be Identification Free!

We are also guided to mention here that Master's do not identify with anything whatsoever and it is part of the path of mastery to release our identifications. Please reflect on this.

List of Common Identifications

We (the personality - soul extension) can identify with:

- **Physical objects:** belongings, things we want to have, objects that surround us and make us feel safe; attachments to objects for the stories they carry.
- **The physical body:** its parts, its sensations and ailments. For example, a carpenter who relies for her work on her hands may identify with her hands and generate attachment there.
- **Thoughts, beliefs, mindset and values:** thoughts generated in the lower mind which we believe in and attach meaning to become part of our identification. These are thoughts which find resonance in the conclusions of our personality throughout lifetimes. From there, we derive our mindsets, values, attitudes and behaviours. As we identify with them, we solidify them in our personality. People with a predominant mental identification find their sense of identity from concepts, ideas, principles...
- **Thought forms:** a thought form is a thought which has taken form as a living energy of its own through the focused intent it has received. It can be nourished by thought repetition or emotion by individuals or a group. The more the repetition of the thought by many people and the inten sity of the emotion they feed it with, the more powerful the thought form. Thought forms make up the collective unconscious of groups.

- **Emotions:** what we feel and what makes us feel alive. People with a predominant identification with the emotional body will find their sense of identity from emotional activity and relationships.
- **Experiences:** memories and ideas of them.
- **Archetypes:** the energetic embodiment of a character type which includes its mindset, polarities, behaviours... For example, "King", "Knight", "Queen", "Maid", "Victim", "Perpetrator", "Lover", "Artist", "Pioneer", "Guardian".
- **Myths and fairy tales:** universal stories which have travelled across times.
- **Religions, institutions, corporations:** Judaism, animism, the Church, the Army, Coca-Cola...
- **Movements:** social, political, philosophical, artistic...

This list is not exhaustive as we can identify with anything really.

Becoming Aware of Your Shadows

Shadow work is another piece of psychological development and integration on your healing journey. Shadow work involves all aspects of self which are rejected, negated and confined to the subconscious mind because you refuse to be identified with them. You deploy considerable energy to not "be it".

Shadows, which are ready to be worked with, are usually just standing in front of you through projections you make onto others. Look for the judgements you hold, especially those which are emotionally charged. As a parent, it is likely that some of these shadows, and usually the most challenging ones, are within your family sphere.

Because shadows are disowned, when they come up, we don't own them and instead point the finger at others: "you did this", "you said this", "you are always like this", "you never do that". In the reflection section of the *Sourceness Journal* we will invite you to reflect upon the shadows you may have with your children.

Parental shadow work is a tender piece of your light path as it will directly touch upon the unworked and unprocessed core of beliefs and challenging experiences you have had as a child and with both masculine and feminine parental figures - this is your relationship with Mother and Father God as the child of God that you are.

The key to unlocking shadow work is to understand that this aspect of Self is not who you are, it is simply a personality construct and touches upon unprocessed experiences. If you continue to negate or reject it, you cannot heal it, and it will persist.

The process we invite you to apply is to look at the shadow with detached observation, from a place of unconditional love and forgiveness. When you shine your loving light onto the shadow, it can be processed. This requires that you can and do look at the shadow face to face with firm unconditional love and listen to it with complete detachment. We propose a process to do shadow work in the *Sourceness Journal*.

Most shadows can be handled in this way. However, some which are linked to trauma and possibly generational issues are more complex to handle. These may need additional healing work and we encourage you to seek competent support with a trauma and shadow work therapist, ideally combined with energy work. Please also read the section on trauma for further input on this.

Recognizing Distortions

For the sake of simplicity, we call the following 'distortions':
- Programs or regenerating programs
- Patterns and habits
- Non-serving energy cords
- Energetic entities
- Spells

Anything which is not in alignment with divine will, which is not serving your highest well-being in this incarnation, which does not benefit of all and which may impact your awareness - conscious or not - and bypass or hijack your willpower, may be considered a distortion.

Distortions can be in any one or more of your bodies, both at personality and soul levels as well as in the spiritual bodies or in the auric field. Distortions in the spiritual bodies often also have a personality level component and need to be cleared there for complete healing.

Self-healing of distortions requires that you can identify them and see them for what they are. Let us look at what each one of them is.

Programs and Regenerating Programs

Like the operating system of a computer, your subconscious mind is programmed through the numerous programs it has received and accepted throughout all your incarnations. Some programs serve you for as long as you need them, and at some point, they become a hindrance to your evolution. When this time comes, they are more like a bug in your system. Some of these programs have never served you, but you have allowed them in, or they were imposed on you.

Programs can impact your physical, emotional and mental states, your worldviews, your sense of self, your spiritual evolution and more. Regeneration/regenerating programs are programs that have been designed to self-regenerate which means that if you clear the program, it will come back unless you clear the regeneration program as well.

These programs are like beliefs which are directly set-up in the grids of your operating system. For example, you can have a control program that commands your relationships, and this causes you to be controlling with your child in everything they do.

Programs are at the root of many of the dissonances we experience at the personality level and when we work with distortions, we will usually find an underlying program associated with it. For example, energy cords between people come into place through a program and without the program they could not attach. Imagine the Tefal pans to which nothing sticks; when you don't have any program in you, nothing can fill up your personality bucket.

Patterns and Habits

Patterns and habits usually stem from programs and are a set of beliefs that have been deeply accepted by you and therefore your lower body system operates without challenging or questioning them. These are all the autopilot functioning's of your personality. For example, through a control program you may have adopted the pattern of checking systematically before you leave the house that the stove is off, the lights are off and the door is locked and come again to recheck. Your conscious mind may consider stepping in to question if this is necessary, however, it will not be given the chance to discuss this point because the pattern under the command of the program is ruling your behaviour.

When the conscious mind gets to the point of seriously questioning this pattern because it has envisaged another way, it will face the resistance of the underlying program beneath the pattern. This usually generates a state of inner struggle. The conscious mind may "win" over the subconscious mind by deploying additional energy to bypass the program/pattern. This can be illustrated by the tremendous efforts people put into diets. They can reach the desired effect so long as the conscious mind is actively on top of the program/pattern but the moment the conscious mind releases its vigilance, the fourth cupcake has been swallowed.

A more effective way would be to clear the program/pattern that causes the issue in the first place - maybe it is an addiction program which expresses itself through a pattern of sugar overeating whenever the emotional body feels lonely.

Habits are exactly like patterns just that they are more systematic in your behaviour. For example, drinking coffee first thing in the morning; reaching for the phone when the mind is idle; getting together with friends on Saturday evenings to drink alcohol and tell jokes; inviting your parents on Sunday for lunch... Habits are automatisms that have been integrated in the personality. As such, they are not more or less difficult than patterns to shift: if you remove the underlying program, patterns and habits lose their foundation.

Energy Cords

All living beings have energy cords between them: we are all connected with one another. When it comes to distortions, we talk about energy cords which are not serving or no longer serving your oversoul in this incarnation. These energy cords are not aligned with divine ideal and divine will and are a hindrance to your evolution.

To the clairvoyant eye, a non-serving energy cord is usually seen as black, red or orange and it links you to someone (a being, entity), whether alive or dead. These cords may be generated from you or may link to you. The problem with non-serving energy cords is that they suck on the energy of the recipient or dump density onto them. When you tune into such a cord in you, you may feel pain and discomfort.

You generate such a cord into someone when you:
- deny your own light and power and seek it in the light and power of someone else.
- disown your own density/baggage and instead of working on transforming it, you dump it on to someone who has a higher light radiance than you do.

- judge someone, for example, someone you have an argument with.
- reject an aspect of creation -for example a shadow or an archetype.

All cords attach to the recipient through a program that they carry within them. For example, for someone to attach an energy cord that sucks on your light to feed their own disempowered state, you must have a program that resonates with it - for example a program which says, "I must help others in need". Clearing these energy cords creates a tremendous inflow of energy back into you. Of course, not all energy cords are limiting. Most of the energy cords we have are based on love and connect us through one another through an energetic fabric of love and unity.

Energetic Entities

Entities are living energies that are consciousness but are not incarnated as you are. They seek the experience of the physical vehicle and as they don't have one themselves, they plug into the physical/energetic body of an incarnated being. There are many ways through which entities come in and some which are referred to as dark entities (not all entities are dark), are screening humanity to enter and inhabit human bodies. It is a bit like a virus: when your immune system is weak, the entity can enter and settle in. if you Pillar of Light is not sealed, they may come in. As long as your Pillar of Light is sealed it is very unlikely that entities will get into your energy system.

Some entities are close to your own vibration range, and they cause minor discomfort; others are so out of balance for your frequency that they can generate illness and disorder. Depending on which of your four / five / 12 / 25 bodies they are anchored in, they will impact you differently:

- Entities which are in the physical body will cause physical pain and illness.
- Entities which are in the etheric body will cause energetic imbalances and eventually affect the physical body.
- Entities which are in the emotional body will cause emotional distress and disorders; and eventually affect the physical body.
- Entities which are in the lower mind will cause mental distress and disorders; and will likely affect the emotional body and eventually the physical body.
- Entities which are in the spiritual bodies affect your spiritual evolution.

If you have never had an energetic clearing, it is highly likely that you have multiple entities within your four lower bodies. If you have done the basic clearing in this book, you will also have cleared numerous entities. If you have chronic pain or a recurring issue that heals when you treat it but then returns, it is also possible that it is related to the impact of an entity.

The point about entities is to understand how they came in: what is the trojan horse within you? There is always a resonance within you that opens the door. Sometimes it is your lack of vigilance and personal power; sometimes it is programs and beliefs within you that make you a suitable ground for the entity. Sometimes, it is through an active spell or enchantment on you that they come in. Sometimes you have had a traumatic event which can unseal your Pillar of Light. Having a well-integrated and sealed Pillar of Light is the best defence against acquiring entities...and just about everything.

If you would like to clear entities from your body, we recommend that you become aware of your programs, patterns and limiting beliefs: there is no point to remove one if you do not clear the underlying trojan horse.

If this is the first time you are reading about entities, it may cause stress: let us normalise that entities are everywhere, and you have lived with them for many incarnations. We all have. To be entirely free from entities will require you to:

- Install, if not already done so, and seal your Pillar of Light
- Do a basic clearing of your Pillar of Light - see the *Sourceness Journal.*
- Fully and definitely stand in your personal power in every Divine Now Moment and clear your own energy system.

For now, it is important that you know they exist. Also, you will find in the *Sourceness Journal* a basic pillar of light clearing exercise.

Spells

There are many structures of spells and enchantments, and it is not needed in this book to go into details about this topic. Again, we would like to draw attention to their existence as they can impact you.

A simple example of a spell is when you say to someone or yourself: "you're so stupid, you will never amount to anything." Especially if your statement is charged with heavy emotions (emotional energy), this will create a condition within you where your subconscious mind will take the order of "being stupid and never amounting to anything" and act on it.

Spells, in our definition, come in two types - there are dark-aligned and light-aligned spells. Dark-aligned spells are conscious energy programs meant to limit or harm someone or block their progress or blocks their free will conscious choice. The actual constitution of a spell, the harmful or blocking constituent, is an energy packet. Dark-aligned spells as made from hatred, jealousy, anger, simple lack of consciousness, allegiance to a group consciousness that is dark-aligned or manipulation by dark-aligned forces. These are the domain of dark magic and are never rooted in love and light. That which is rooted in love and light, .i.e. spells etc. are referred to as white magic. If you feel, sense, see or know you are impacted by a spell, please know that you have likely triggered it or your soul has agreed to it for the purpose of the experience your soul seeks. If you have cast a spell on someone, there is likely a non-aligned energy cord with the other person(s). These may be removed. Whether you have been the recipient of a spell or the caster of it, we recommend you practise forgiveness. There are examples for forgiveness practise in the *Sourceness Journal.*

Chapter 3
Balancing Polarity

We have already mentioned that the personality level operates through polarity. Polarity is two opposing forces which represent each one of the two sides of the same coin. The Balancing of Polarity refers to the inherent balance or equilibrium within our human energy of these opposing forces.

Everything in the Universe is Source (All That Is), however, within the human energy system we must balance a polarity of divine feminine and divine masculine energy.

When we talk about divine feminine and divine masculine energies, we are not talking about biological sex nor identity. We are referring to the polarity at the spiritual level of our beingness.

The polarity energies are regulated - and that is a less-than-ideal word - through the sacral chakra. The second chakra - sacral chakra - is also known as the polarity chakra - it is important to integrate the two polarities of male and female, right and left side of this chakra:
- Right - might - male
- Left - female.

When the personality / sacral chakra is not balanced we experience inner conflict and mis-alignment (which eventually manifests as outer conflict). You will find further exercises in the *Sourceness Journal* and meditations to balance polarity within you as well as heal issues related to the divine feminine and the divine masculine.

Process: Balancing Polarity

Standing with your knees slightly bent, reach up with your left hand, palm up, above your head. Visualise the full moon with rays of its pale white light flooding down through your hand and down the left side of your body into the earth. Feel this flow for about a minute.

Gently lower your left hand and raise your right hand to the same position above your head. Visualise the Sun flooding rays of its golden light into your hand and down the right side of your body into the earth.

After about a minute, again raise both hands, and feel both flowing at the same time, the moonlight through your left hand and down the left side, the sunlight through your right hand and down the right side.

If one side feels more powerful than the other, increase the energy on the other side until it feels balanced.

After about a minute, lower both hands, place your palms together and turn them inward so that your fingers are touching the centre of your chest.

Visualise a balanced flow of light from both hands flowing into your heart chakra and energising your whole system.[xiv]

Chapter 4
Parenting Your Inner Child and Divine Child

Every oversoul is a "child of God". We refer to the child within at the soul level, as the Divine Child - Divine Feminine - Divine Masculine mirroring Inner Child - Inner Feminine - Inner Masculine. Let's look at what both mean and why they are important on your parenting journey.

At the Personality Level

Within every adult, there is also a child. As a parent you have the responsibility of your children, but also of your own inner child. You really parent your children only as well as you parent yourself. As you grow up and become an adult yourself, your parents no longer have responsibility over you: instead, you have the responsibility over all aspects of you and this includes the child within. No matter how grown up you are, there is always a child aspect in your personality that needs your attention.

For most people, the experience of childhood has not been ideal in most incarnations. Inner child work is about going back to your childhood to heal the wounds of the past held within your subconscious mind and personality by releasing old hurts and limiting beliefs and bringing unconditional love where it was missing. Issues related to the inner child also involve the hurts and wounds related to Mother and Father. As you are an adult yourself, the healing process of the inner child involves the healing of the trinity: Mother, Father & Child.

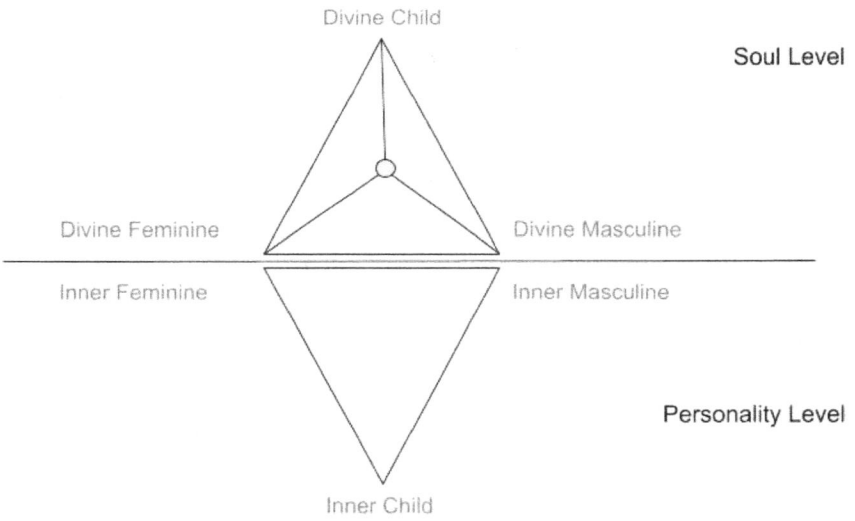

Diagram 19. Divine Child and Inner Child

If you have unprocessed issues which go back to your childhood, then it is important that you dedicate part of your inner work to heal your inner child. Childhood issues may not only be related to this incarnation: whichever issue from other lives that you have not resolved will remain within your personality bucket until you address them. Conclusions you have drawn in other lives which may have been helpful then, and may no longer be relevant to this current incarnation, need updating/clearing.

A healthy inner child knows it is loved; it feels safe and free to explore the world and bond with others; it is in touch with its natural innocence and relies on its inner resources. Your work as an adult is to tend to your inner child and ensure it is healthy in your personality.

When the inner child becomes healthy, meaning you are parenting it with firm unconditional love and fulfilling ideally your inner roles of Mother and Father, then you can access the divine child within you at the soul level.

How do we Know our Inner Child is Wounded?

We direct you to the *Sourceness Journal* for exercises and information about how to know what woundings your inner child may have.

Woundings manifest in behaviours and patterns of thinking which do not serve us.

Here we list common outcomes of inner child woundings in the personality level:

1. Co-dependence

Characterised by a loss of identity. Being out of touch with one's feelings, needs and desires. If one has no sense of where one ends and another begins, this can be an indication of co-dependence wounds.

2. Offender behaviours

The wounded inner child may express as quiet and long-suffering, or violent and cruel, and everything in between. Overindulgence and over submission, so that children learn to feel that they are superior to others is also offender behaviour. This is now commonly referred to as 'entitled' behaviour. A sense of entitlement is a personality trait that is based on a person's belief that the world owes them something in exchange for nothing; that they deserve something even though they haven't earned it—recognition, rewards, good grades, or a promotion. They see only their needs as important, and often feel the rules don't apply to them.

3. Narcissistic disorders

Every one of us was a we before we became an I. The narcissistically deprived inner child contaminates the parent/child constellation with an insatiable craving for love, attention and affection.

4. Trust issues

When caregivers are untrustworthy, children develop a deep sense of distrust. Their world seems a dangerous, hostile and unsafe place. The child concludes that they must always be on guard and in control. They come to believe that 'If I control everything, then no one can hurt me.' a control mechanism develops, and control can become an addiction or obsession.

5. Acting out / Acting in behaviours

Acting out refers to the unconscious expression of repressed emotions or unresolved conflicts through impulsive or disruptive behaviour - often occurs without conscious awareness or understanding of its root causes.

Acting in behaviour refers to a subset of personality disorder traits that are more self-destructive than outwardly destructive.

6. Magical thinking

Magical thinking is the belief that one's ideas, thoughts, actions, words, or use of symbols can influence the course of events in the material world. It presumes a causal link between one's inner, personal experience and the external physical world. A person may literally believe in magic or supernatural forces, or they may simply worry that their inner life could influence the world in unexpected ways.

7. Intimacy dysfunctions

Some people find it quite difficult to share their feelings with their partner. This fear often is not restricted to emotions, but also to being physically intimate. Intimacy disorder, or intimacy anxiety disorder, is when the individual fears to be too close to other people and especially the one they love. They can't get involved physically or emotionally with them.

8. Undisciplined behaviours

Undisciplined behaviour refers to a lack of self-control, order, or adherence to rules or regulations. It is characterised by failure to maintain a structured approach in actions, behaviours, or decision-making processes. Undisciplined behaviour can be wilful and not properly controlled, leading to flagrant violations of norms and regulations, culminating in chaos and disorder.

9. Addictive compulsive behaviours

Compulsive behaviour plays a role in the addiction process. As an addiction develops, it often will involve a feeling of compulsion to take an addictive substance, such as alcohol or heroin, or to carry out an addictive behaviour, such as gambling or sex.

10.   Thought distortions

There are many different thought distortions, also referred to as cognitive distortions. Cognitive distortions are biassed perspectives that we take on ourselves and the world around us. They are irrational thoughts and beliefs that we unknowingly reinforce over time.

These patterns and systems of thought are often subtle - it's difficult to recognize them when they are a regular feature of your day-to-day thoughts. That is why they can be so damaging since it's hard to change what you don't recognize as something that needs to change!

11.   Emptiness (apathy, depression)

Depression is a mood disorder that results in persistent feelings of sadness, emptiness, or hopelessness. Other symptoms may include sleep disturbances, energy and appetite changes, guilty feelings, and suicidal thoughts. Conversely, people with apathy, lack interest in, or motivation for, the activities that they usually enjoy.

At the Soul Level

Working with the divine child is going within to connect directly with your oversoul. The divine inner child is the truest, purest, wisest part of us that always lives within our heart. This child is all-believing and filled with divine trust, love and faith. The divine child is our oversoul's expression of who we are and what we came to do, before the current world we are incarnated into got a hold of us and domesticated us, before our parents and society moulded us. Every human being living on the planet has an oversoul and therefore a divine inner child. The divine child within has a very strong connection with Ray 9.

When we are disconnected from our divine inner child, we are not acknowledging our divinity and the sacred journey that our oversoul is on in this incarnation. Disconnection can make us feel like:

- We do not know what we want in life,
- We never feel true satisfaction or joy in our daily lives,
- We are working to survive and never really living.

Disconnection can also cause you to believe that your value is based on something outside of you, such as material possessions you have, your physical good looks, the money in your bank account, or the beautiful person who is your partner.

This allowing the outside world to tell you what you are prevents you from experiencing your own unique expression of divinity to flow through you. None of these outside external things will truly ignite your spirit or set your heart on fire, at least not for long.

The path of external identification leads to experiencing that there is always something else to accomplish or acquire. In the end, it leads to a feeling of inner emptiness. We've all been there because we've all grown up in a world that praises the external not the internal.

As an adult, your divine inner child can help you wake up and reconnect to the glory that you truly are. What can you expect when you start to connect with your divine inner child? Lots! When we connect with our divine child within and allow that child to bring us back to our truest self, we raise our vibrations and expand. We begin to see that the world doesn't tell us who we are, we shout out to the world "this is what I AM!". This is incredibly empowering. Going within your own heart allows you to put what the world wants from you aside and helps you to clearly see - this is what brings me joy!

Human beings are unique expressions of Source, and everyone brings a special gift, perspective, energy or vibration to the world. No one can be you, no one can live for you, and no one can express your unique Source expression! Your divine child knows what your soul sent you to this life to accomplish. Connecting with this child can help you get insight on your true passions, give you the encouragement and guidance you need to create the life of your dreams, and fully express the uniqueness that is you. The energy shift that you will feel from within is just incredible. In this sense, you can experience your childhood in the here and now. Most importantly, let your divine inner child show you how to play and truly enjoy what human life has to offer. We are here to enjoy life!

As a parent, and at the current stage of human evolution, you cannot prevent your children from being drawn to the outer excitements of life and experiencing the wants and desires of their personality. What you can do is to carefully watch where the moulding of society, mass consciousness and consensus reality, as well as your own inner child unprocessed issues, impact your child in a way which is creating disconnection to their divine child within.

As a parent, you have the double job of re-awakening your connection to your own divine child and maintaining the connection of your child to their divine child within. If you tune into the divine child of your child and observe it, it will most likely help you in your own re-awakening process. Especially in the very early years when your child is at home with you and is not yet highly exposed to the moulding of society, you can create spaces of free exploration for your child and observe with detached non-judgemental observation and loving kindness the divine child embodies by your child.

Chapter 5
Source and Sourceness

This book is prepared under the guidance of Ascended Masters and is directly connected to our individual service to Source. A foundation of this book is the healing of your divine connection to oversoul, monad and ultimately Source. For this to occur, it is also necessary to clarify what we mean by Source.

What do we Mean by Source?

We do not wish to impress any 'truth' upon those who read this book. We seek to provide helpful constructive and practical suggestions and solutions for an energetic world, much of which is almost entirely invisible and intangible to most people and this is no judgement.

Even if you cannot yet grasp it, but you are willing to consider that we live in a world of energy, where we are surrounded by energy flowing in multiple ways at multiple times and spaces, then we invite you to feel, sense, see, know, hear our suggestions.

Our starting point is that everything is energy. We are energy. All around and permeating through us is energy which doesn't come from anywhere and doesn't go anywhere, it is already here in a continuous process of movement and evolution.

All the energy in the world comes from Undifferentiated Source expressing itself and seeking to experience itself as energy. Our guides have stressed the word undifferentiated to point out that all energy that has ever been and will ever be is Source. Undifferentiated Source is pure energy that exists. It is. It is all that is. It is everywhere, in everything, is everything. As Undifferentiated Source expands, the Universe expands... which is also what scientists have recognized.

Source has also been called God. We, each of us, has been given a spark of this pure energy and the spark (which contains all of God/Source) that we are is a level of our being which we are mostly unconscious of (referred to as the monadic level). This spark of divine essence is God/Source. It is God/Source. There is nothing else for this spark to be but God/Source.

The spark of God is the monadic level. The sparking process from God is like a flow of sourceness which evolves and waves. The beginning of the sparking process occurs when the male sperm fertilises the female egg. Scientifically it has been shown that fireworks of energy are emitted by this fusion.

Source is pure energy which may be identified as vast, unconfined, unlimited energy spreading through and in our Universe. Energy may be transformed, transmuted, balanced, restored but we, in our present state of consciousness, may not destroy or create it.

God/Source is constantly evolving. It is not static energy. It is moving and evolving. We as an individual spark (or monad) are in the process of collecting data, information, wisdom, mostly of a spiritual nature (unseeable for most part) about what Source is. Until you have reached the soul merge where your personality or lower self has fully surrendered to soul, you are mostly unaware of this quest and activity of your soul.

For our purposes we ask you to allow this impression of Source as pure energy in the process of experiencing itself to be an option for you. It may not be your truth, and that's okay. But if it is a possibility, then the suggestions we have in this book will greatly assist you and your child to make sense of the energetic environment, some might call it, an energetic ocean, in which we exist, live and breathe.

What do we Mean by Sourceness?

Source, although deeply and profoundly who we are, is not graspable to the personality. At best, the personality can create ideas and beliefs about it - and it has. The more anchored you are in your personality; the more Source is a concept that the mind will want to understand if you have an interest in spirituality. This is counterproductive and will develop what is commonly called the spiritual ego: identification with spiritual beliefs. Instead of helping your mind develop ideas, concepts, beliefs... about Source, our Guides have strongly emphasised the word sourceness to be used instead to avoid this trap.

Sourceness is the experience of Source in this Divine Now Moment. If you try to explain or understand Source, you are in your mind and not experiencing Source. If you are looking for words to speak about Source or describe it, you are restricting Source and not experiencing Source.

Sourceness is about being in the now. Parenting as a Light Path is about embodying your unique expression of Source in this very Divine Now Moment. At the oversoul level and beyond, you can experience Source, feel Source, be Source and this is the purpose of this book: that everyone is able to experience their unique sourceness.

Denial of Source

Every human being currently incarnated has had a traumatic experience at some point of their soul journey, related to the separation from Source with resulting core limiting beliefs and programs which are impeding their ability to experience Source fully.

If you are rejecting, negating, denying, suppressing Source in your life, then we invite you to investigate your core wounds of separation, abandonment, humiliation, rejection, unworthiness, distrust and your core fears. You will find in the *Sourceness Journal* exercises to explore your denial of Source and repair this fundamental link. The most important relationship in your life is your connection with yourself, and by this we mean your unique divine blueprint, your God-self.

A Message from Source

Dear One, you are a divine being and the entire universe is contained within you.

You are Source experiencing itself through the infinite and multidimensional possibilities of life which I, as the I-amness which we are, am experiencing with and through you. I am that I am. I am all that I am. Everything is within me, by me and through me. There is no separation between anything nor anyone. There is only what IS. I am grateful for the experiences you enable me to experience. All is my divine will.

However, you are entrusted with a very special choice that enables your unique experience on Earth and that is your free will. This enables you to go against me, to experiment outside of my Divine Plan, to live the infinite possibilities of Creation. In recent years, your experimentation has become dull and constricted: you have solidified beyond the Divine Plan certain beliefs and identifications which are severely thinning your experience of who you truly are. Some of you have imposed your views on others, diminishing further their potential to return to Me. All of that is also Me but now, my Will is not to support this.

You are creating limitations that impact the entire human species, other species on Earth and Earth itself. I am willing a new evolution on Earth. I am willing that human beings reclaim their power and return to Me. I am making available all the help that is needed for all those who are ready to follow the path back to their God-self Light and Unconditional Love. The decision is with you.

May Divine Love, Light, Wisdom and Power guide you.

October 3rd 2023

Challenges Arise

As you set the intention and begin the practice of cultivating divine qualities, as you set your intention towards soul merge or simply in your daily life, you will notice that challenges arise as if something was in the way and blocking the path.

Some of the blockers:
- Limiting beliefs which are deeply ingrained in your subconscious mind.
- Programs installed in your body system - some of which may be inherited through your ancestral line, from your childhood experience or other lives, and from consciousness groups connected with you.
- Emotional blockages such as unprocessed or suppressed emotions.
- Energetic blockages you have taken over or created - which may be yours or not.
- Memories of previous experiences which are painful.
- Trauma - physical, emotional or mental.
- Archetypal energies that shape your personality and which are no longer serving you.
- Impact of psychic attacks on your body system.

For example, as you start to cultivate trust, you may experience a refusal from your body system to surrender to the divine, or a fear of relying on God, or a feeling of abandonment or betrayal. Detached observation will help you notice what is happening within you. The next step is clearing the blockage and resetting to your divine blueprint. To use the analogy of gardening, clearing and enabling your body system to return to its divine blueprint is like weeding your garden, preparing the soil to grow the plants you want to have in your garden and planting new seeds.

It is also worthwhile mentioning that healing and evolution are not fully in your hands: you oversee setting the intention and divine will and timing play their part. You may become aware that there is a blockage in you, but if it's not in alignment with divine will and timing to clear this now, it is ideal for your
highest well-being to wait until it is. There are multiple reasons, and we can list a few for your understanding:

- You have a soul commitment to another soul, and it is necessary for your evolutionary journey to keep a program and belief even if it causes discomfort for you.
- You have not yet learned the full lesson your soul seeks.
- You have not allowed your emotional body to express itself or integrate the learning.
- There is another piece of healing which needs to happen first.
- You have not yet gained the wisdom to understand the role the perceived blockage is playing in your life.

These are just some examples. Acceptance and surrenderedness are very useful qualities to face such a situation; also, you can ask for comfort and know that it is always divine will for you to heal eventually but you may not understand it fully. However, we would like to stress that you have a big role to play by thoroughly examining your belief system, agreements, vows, loyalties... to make sure that you are not carrying limitations.

Shifting beliefs is always your responsibility and when something is in the way, it is fair to first do everything in your power to shift it. The quality of trust and wonder are also helpful to infuse your own healing process with curiosity and faith. You may see the belief as an obstacle, a challenge, a game which you can be sure you will win, somehow in a time and space which may not be known to you now, but the outcome of winning is certain. Does this remind you of a quality? Yes, it is the playfulness attitude!

There are multiple tools in the *Sourceness Journal* which you can use to do your clearing and healing work. Please know that this work is not something you do first and then you can master the qualities. Everything is part of your life; your Light Path and we are never really done with our clearing and healing work. The more we integrate, the more we progress in our ability to be Light and radiate the Light that we are (the higher our Light Radiance), the more subtle our clearing and healing work becomes.

When challenges arise, we can be grateful for their gift. The era we are in is that of delimited-ness and it involves the work of clearing our limitations. If we can approach this work with gratitude, we can also enjoy the journey.

Conclusion

We started this book by mentioning that everyone is a parent. As we are now concluding it, we realise that being an integrated soul extension is all about parenting: it is the verb which describes what it means to become an adult, to serve others, to care for the child in you, or to care for those you are responsible for in your family, profession or community.

Every oversoul is a child of Source and being an oversoul means parenting the 12 soul extensions which make it. Whether or not it is in your responsibility to integrate the 12 soul extensions in your oversoul, you are still part of this process and at the oversoul level, you are made of 12 soul extensions. In this sense, the adults of today indeed have something to learn from the children, who come into the world with a (partial) soul merge: it is already ingrained in their being-ness to care for and parent one another.

Golden Earth is based on this understanding: humanity is not about being realised individuals; it is a collective experience which relies on parenting. The principles of (even modern) parenting which disregard the soul level are not relevant for the Golden Earth; nor are the principles of education, economy, politics… which our societies are resting upon.

It is a completely new operating model based on a new understanding of what it means to be a whole human, a realised God-self which is required; the topics discussed, and the energetic codes shared in this book are setting these new foundations. Sourceness is the foundation of Golden Earth, and a new era is upon us. It starts with our personal spiritual work and our collective realisation of our inherent interconnectedness, inter-beingness.

i	Grattan, Brian. *(1994) Mahatma I & II: The I Am Presence* (p. 223). Light Technology Publishing. Arizona, USA. Kindle Edition.
ii	Grattan, Brian. (1994) *Mahatma I & II: The I Am Presence (p. 550).* Light Technology Publishing. Arizona, USA. Kindle Edition.
iii	Grattan, Brian. (1994) *Mahatma I & II: The I Am Presence* (p. 332). Light Technology Publishing. Arizona, USA. Kindle Edition.
iv	Grattan, Brian. *(1994) Mahatma I & II: The I Am Presence (p. 108).* Light Technology Publishing. Arizona, USA. Kindle Edition.
v	Grattan, Brian. (1994) *Mahatma I & II: The I Am Presence* (pp. 106-107). Light Technology Publishing. Arizona, USA. Kindle Edition.
vi	Grattan, Brian. (1994) *Mahatma I & II: The I Am Presence* (pp. 71-72). Light Technology Publishing. Arizona, USA. Kindle Edition.
vii	Brennan, Barbara Ann. (1993) *Light Emerging: The Journey of Personal Healing.* Bantam Books, London.
viii	Light Omega Newsletter community@lightomega.org -Sept. 20, 2023.
ix	When we talk about illusions, glamour and maya we refer to the definition offered by Dr Joshua David Stone: these refer to three levels of delusion. Glamour is delusion which refer to the emotional plane; Illusion is delusion which refers to the mental plane; Maya is delusion which refers to the etheric plane. We refer you to chapter 6 on this topic in Dr Joshua David Stone's book, *The Complete Ascension Manual: How to Achieve Ascension in this Lifetime.* Light Technology Publishing. Arizona, USA. 1994.
x	Grattan, Brian. (1994). *Mahatma I & II: The I Am Presence* (pp. 548-549). Light Technology Publishing. Arizona, USA. Kindle Edition.
xi	Brennan, Barbara Ann. (1993) *Light Emerging: The Journey of Personal Healing.* Bantam Books, London.
xii	https://www.brainyquote.com/quotes/antoine_de_saintexupery_101532
xiii	Stone, Joshua David. (1994) *The Complete Ascension Manual: How to Achieve Ascension in this Lifetime.* Light Technology Publishing. Arizona, USA. Kindle Edition.
xiv	Adapted from Brian Grattan (1994) *Mahatma I & II: The I Am Presence.* Light Technology Publishing. Arizona, USA. Kindle Edition.

Overview of the Sourceness Series

At the time of publishing, we have clarity about the following books and guides which are in the process of channeling / publishing in the Sourceness Series.

Sourceness: A Series for Golden Earth Being

Parenting - Book One:

This is the first book we have been tasked to write and it is intended for all adults, including parents on their path of parenting - this involves their own inner child but also their physical children. It is a complete manual to the process of soul merge and addresses the oversoul.

Parenting - *Sourceness Journal*:

This journal accompanies Parenting and offers exercises, meditations, practices, reflections, enquiries and suggestions to support the guidance offered in Parenting - Book One.

Nurturing - Book Two:

This is the second book we have been tasked to write in the Sourceness series and it is focused on the monadic merge. It is intended for all people who are undergoing or completing soul merge. It addresses the monad. We dive into the three aspects of nurturing: sustaining, caring for and protecting and this includes humanity and Earth.

Constellating - Book Three:

This book addresses the group monad level and is intended for all those who are working towards their planetary monadic merge and galactic monadic merge.

Expanding - Book Four:

This book addresses the planetary and galactic monadic levels and is intended for all those who are working towards cosmic monadic merge.

Generating - Book Five:

This book addresses the multi-universal monadic merge and is intended for all those who are called to integrate this level.

There are seven further books to be channeled in the Sourceness series.

Parenting - Oversoul Guides

These 12 channeled guides are addressing specific topics related to Parenting - Book One in greater detail and are intended for those who are new to the spiritual path and working towards or completing oversoul merge. The guides can be read in any order. We recommend that you follow your guidance as to which one to read first.

The Golden Earth - Guide 1

Preparing our transition towards Golden Earth by calling it forth within our consciousness and aligning to it at oversoul and personality levels.

Divine Power - Guide 2

Establishing what is divine power, how to 'stand in it', how it is different from personal power, and how and why it is part of the oversoul experience. Tools and practices to align to one's divine ideal power.

The Vibrant Personality - Guide 3

Our manual to live a vibrant life at the personality level and prepare the personality for the oversoul merge and oversoul being.

Protecting Self and Space - Guide 4

Protecting oneself against non-serving energies, psychic attacks and entities. Clearing, cleaning and upgrading one's space so that it protects and supports.

Sensitivity - Guide 5

An introduction to subtle sensing through the lens of high sensitivity, empathy and compassion.

Integrated Channel - Guide 6

A guide to becoming an integrated channel, hone one's subtle sensing skills and progressing on the path of Sourceness. Integrated channeling supports our mission work and the work of all.

Death - Guide 7

An overview of the death processes, the purpose of death and how to navigate death throughout our incarnations as an oversoul. This guide also includes support to live through the experience of death in this lifetime as is divine ideal in alignment with divine will.

Bodies of Light - Guide 8

An oversoul focused guide to the development, realization and nurturing of Bodies of Light - divine light structures - that are relevant to all oversoul constellations, Earth and Source.

Rays and Radiance - Guide 9

An introduction to the divine technology of the 12 Rays of Source, how to work with them on one's sourceness journey and how to activate, enhance, constellate and generate radiance.

Coherent Living - Guide 10

A guide to living in coherence at personality and oversoul level.

Clearing and Healing self and Self - Guide 11

An introduction for oversoul level clearing and healing.

The Divine Mind - Guide 12

An introduction to the mind of Source, how to anchor one's mind in the divine mind and manifest sourceness. Tools and practices for integrating the subconscious and conscious mind with the divine mind.